YOU MADE IT...
NOW SELL IT!!!

THE ULTIMATE GUIDE TO SELLING YOUR
HANDMADE JEWELRY

BY SUSIE EDWARDS

Long Beach, California
www.pudgypublishing.com

You made it...Now sell it!!

The ultimate guide to selling your handmade jewelry

You Made It...Now Sell It!!! The ultimate guide to selling your handmade Jewelry/Susie Bradford Edwards, author.

Includes index.

ISBN/10 0-9649887-0-4
ISBN/13 978-0-9649887-0-5
First printing, 2007
Second printing, 2008

Printed in United States by

PO Box 21082
Long Beach, CA 90801
562-427-0018

Send e-mails to: info@pudgypublishing.com
To download PDF forms visit our Web site @ www.pudgypublishing.com

ҩ҂ҩ҂ҩ҂ҩ҂

DEDICATIONS AND ACKNOWLEDGEMENTS:

To my mother Aretha, who taught me the true meaning of hard work and showed me by her examples how to take sour lemons and make sweet lemonade.

To my Husband Scott, you are my inspiration and the one person who truly gets me, supports me, and encourages me…. you are my rock. Without you this book definitely would not be possible, I love you.

Thank you to my editor, Mary Nesfield. You surfaced in my life at just the right time. Your expertise and professionalism was needed and absolutely appreciated.

Thank you to my dear friend Carli Steers, who is all about spreading positive energy and love.

Thanks to all the teachers who nurtured me, encouraged me, enlightened me and told me that I could be whatever I could dream.

A big thanks to my many customers who have become my friends who I have helped mentor and direct into their own successful jewelry businesses…I have learned from you too…Thanks!

CONTENTS

MY STORY

One question I'm always asked, is how did I get into beads and designing jewelry? My relationship with art started in childhood, which led to my majoring in art in college. After getting married and becoming a devoted wife and mother, I realized I had lost myself in the process. I never dreamed that I would find what I so desperately needed in a vintage necklace that had been my mother's. The beads were truly beautiful but the necklace was in desperate need of repair. Knowing absolutely nothing about how to put a broken necklace back together, I went to the library and found a book on jewelry making. A few days later I had a beautiful necklace and a pair of earrings. That's all it took to know that I had finally found my true passion.

Making jewelry allowed me to utilize all the things I'd learned in my art classes, like color, balance, light, harmony etc. I started examining all the pieces of jewelry I had in my jewelry box and decided that I would discover all there was to know about designing. I found a local bead store, which was really hard to find at the time, and it became my second home.

I poured my heart and soul into my jewelry. The compliments I got boosted my self esteem and gave me confidence that I didn't know I had. Eventually I started selling a few of my creations to friends and relatives. It wasn't long before I decided to see if I could make money with my designs. Even in the beginning, I knew that transferring what I loved into money would not be easy.

Using vintage beads and Swarovksi crystals as primary components, one piece at a time, I labored over my first line that I tore apart and reassembled at least a dozen times before I had a style that I loved. It wasn't easy keeping myself motivated without any outside positive reinforcement. Believing in yourself and your dream is hardest in the beginning stages of converting your passion into a business. This is when you have to breathe it, imagine it, feel it and desire it almost every waking moment. At those low inspiration points when my beads and what I was making with them weren't talking to me, I would draw on my dream and it always got me through.

In the end my line consisted of 40 necklaces and earrings. I knew early on that I wanted to manufacture a wholesale production line. I wanted my jewelry in Nordstrom's, which was one of my favorite stores, but had no idea how I would do it. In my quest to market my jewelry, I was told about a professional jewelry show at the Los Angeles Convention Center that I signed up for. It was at that show that I not only picked up several high-end boutique accounts but I met and hired my first rep. She simply adored my jewelry and gave me pointers on pricing and perfecting my line; I will always be indebted to her for helping me find my way.

A year later, my rep became ill and retired from representing designers, but I was up and running by then. She'd gotten my jewelry into some of Los Angeles' top boutiques, including many in Beverly Hills and Hollywood, so finding a new rep with my track record was fairly easy. As destiny would have it, I signed on with one of the most sought-after reps in Los Angeles. The rep got my jewelry to numerous celebrities and television shows, including several soap opera television shows and Starsearch, which was a talent search show. Before long I was featured in major magazines and my dream of seeing my items in Nordstrom's, Saks, Horchow catalog, Neiman's, Cache and many upscale boutiques was realized. Eventually I grew my business into a half-million-dollar business a year.

The huge learning curve I mastered was filled with numerous scrapes, bumps and falls, but I not only survived…I thrived. My staff grew to over 20 employees and the vision I'd had for my business became a reality. It is my hope that this book and my experience can help guide you into a successful jewelry career or whatever your desires are with your jewelry.

Sincerely,
Susie Bradford Edwards

INTRODUCTION

Thank you for purchasing *"You Made It...Now Sell It."* My accessory design career was created not only from passion but need. I believe that when passion and need meet you will find success. That's not to say, that one without the other cannot meet the same end, but definitely when ignited, they will create a fire that is hard to put out.

This book was written to help newcomers and veterans of the costume jewelry trade sell their jewelry. I'll show you how to find the perfect rep, how to choose a winning showroom and how to sell online with and without a Web site. You will also find invaluable information on landing your own boutique accounts and what you absolutely must know before doing consignment. This book is meant to be a reference guide to help you turn your passion for creating jewelry into a profitable business. The information in this book is based on over 18 years of experience in the costume jewelry industry. I will expose you to potential problems of working with major department stores and offer you viable solutions. Our resource pages are filled with tons of industry contact information that you will refer to time and time again. We've even included sample forms, and on our Web site you can download blank forms for your personal use.

If money is needed to get your business off the ground, we'll explore avenues you probably haven't thought of to secure funds. We will help you avoid costly mistakes by taking you through the entire process of making and selling your jewelry. It is my hope that this book will help guide and drive your passion into whatever success you want your jewelry business to become.

ఌఐఌఐఌఐఌఐఌఐ

Inspirational Quote: "If you don't know where you are going, you'll end up someplace else," Yogi Berra

CHAPTER 1

ARE YOU REALLY READY?

Passion is one thing, but to turn your passion into business will require you to be "all about business." Many people dream of turning their passion into a business, but making the transition will take lots of persistence and determination. The true reality is that doing so will require sacrifice and hard work; but if your goal is to transform your dreams into money, then this book will help you make the right decisions. I'm sure you already receive many compliments from the jewelry you make. You may even have sold a few pieces, so it's only natural that you should start to think about the next step, which is turning your hobby into a business. Ask almost anyone and they will tell you that they want to be their own boss, to steer their own ship or paddle their own canoe. Words are easy, but it's entirely another matter to put power, determination and follow-through behind those words and actually do it. The first question you should answer is, "What do you want your new business to do for you? Support you, because you need it? Supplement your income, because you want to purchase extras or take a great vacation? Get admiration from friends and family? Provide for you when you retire? Your answer will determine just how much or how little work you want to put into your new business.

Start your new venture by doing some creative visualization. Do you see your jewelry in a chain of retail stores like Neiman's or Macy's? Do you see yourself telling your boss goodbye and making jewelry full time? Or do you just see yourself selling enough of your jewelry to cover the costs of your habit and get accolades from people around you? Take a pen and paper and write down your dream. I want you to see and think your dream constantly.

Now that you have your future in clear focus, I want you to throw in a dash of reality. How much time do you have to invest in your new venture? How much money? How do you feel about selling and marketing? How good are you at details like bookkeeping? As you can see making and selling your jewelry will become a real business with traditional business issues. Finding the right balance of creative design time and managing the requirements of the business part of your venture is challenging for the novice or the experienced jewelry artist. Balancing what's required to design, produce and sell your product involves prioritizing and compromising between your passion and business. Ask yourself; will you enjoy your passion when it becomes your work? If your hobby becomes your business, you will be required to balance administrative duties with creative time. Spending your time overseeing production, sales and paperwork can seem overwhelming. Even if you have someone else handling all your business issues, you should still know exactly what's going on with your business... after all it is your business. Be warned that you will have to make some drastic decisions and your life as you know it will change. Working for yourself will involve working twelve-to fifteen-hour days as opposed to working an eight-hour job. Only you can decide if your desire is greater than the sacrifice you will have to make. Depending on your personality you will either rise to the challenge or become overwrought with a case of nerves. You might find your creative energies flowing and open or blocked and shut down. Early on you won't have much positive reinforcement so keeping your dream alive will have to come from the fire within.

One thing you will need above all else is that you have to be a self-starter. Remember if you don't start it, nurture it and keep it going, it won't go.

MAJOR POINTS TO CONSIDER BEFORE THE COMMITMENT:

You should consider just what you will need before starting your home-based jewelry business, and answer the following four questions:

1. Can you make a transition from home to business during the work hours you set for yourself and from business to home during off hours?

2. Can you deal with the isolation of working from home?

3. Are you disciplined enough to set and meet work schedules without a boss?

4. Are you ready for your relationship with jewelry making to change?

When answering the first two questions keep in mind that the amount of discipline you have will play a huge role in your success. Will you use your time wisely and constructively? Working from home will be filled with many distractions, the dishes, the laundry, etc. Can you ignore the chores that need to be done and structure your day as if you were at work away from home?

You will have to set a realistic work schedule and stick firmly to it. I also want you to be just as disciplined about ending your workday. This is really important because if you don't set boundaries you may find yourself facing burnout. I know it's hard not to run to your home office to pick up a phone call, check your e-mail or read a fax that just came in after you've ended your business day, but I know that with practice you can do it, and at whatever time your workday resumes you can pick up where you left off.

In answer to question four, I do want you to know that when you make the transition from hobby to business, your relationship with designing your jewelry will change. In some ways you may be freer with your designing because you will design things with items that you might not choose for yourself. In other ways you will become more restrictive because you will have to pay attention to what you pay for items you use because you will be reselling them.

TIPS TO HELP YOU GET ON THE RIGHT ROAD:

- If you do not have a day job, I do want you to prepare for work…take your shower, get dressed and prepare for work just as you would if you were working outside of your home.

- I do want you to be firm and not let friends or family sabotage your workday. Make them realize that just because you're working at home doesn't mean that they can show up without you knowing they are coming. If you don't stand firm you'll get elected to do whatever errands or chores family members need done during the day on a regular basis.

- I'm assuming you already have the support of your family members because having this business will change their lives as well. Hopefully you have a partner who can help provide you with some financial and emotional stability. Remind your family that you will definitely have new demands on your time and you will need their support. Of course the plus side of this for everyone is that you will be making your dreams come true and that translates into everyone being happier.

- I do want you to ask yourself if you are the kind of person who can forgive your mistakes and there will be many, especially as your business grows. As with anything successful, your business will evolve and require changes and with that comes uncertainty. Because you are always crossing hurdles you haven't crossed before you will develop confidence in your ability to face the challenges and to ride out your mistakes. Just keep in mind that successful business owners learn from their mistakes. Then you can proceed, basking in the knowledge that they have crossed a bridge they won't have to cross again.

- I do want you to let your voicemail answer your phone during your workday. Chatting on the phone, even with well meaning friends can wreck your work schedule.

- I do want you to treat your new business work studio as a separate entity from the rest of your house. Whether you are using a garage, basement, or a spare room as your studio space, I want you to maintain a professional environment. No bedrooms or corners in the kitchen please. These don't afford you privacy or separate your space from the rest of the house. You will need a more permanent solution. Claiming a space where you can leave your designs in progress out without having to shove them out of the way for dinner should be your goal.

- I do want your business to have its own phone, landline or cell. You should also have a mailing address and a separate business bank account. This makes tax time much less complicated and it will appear to the IRS that you are a real business versus someone playing business.

- I do want you to be aware of Federal, State and Local regulations. Finding out this information is important when considering what type of business you can run from your home.

- I do want you to respect your neighbors and the type of neighborhood you live in. By having a home-based jewelry business, more than likely you'll have increased traffic from either your clients, suppliers, work force or mail services. I moved my home-based business from my house when it became obvious that I was running a real business. I had regular UPS drop-offs and pickups in the morning and afternoons and a staff of girls coming and going in the morning, at lunch and leaving in the evenings, along with boyfriends or husbands picking them up.

- I do want you to do some basic realistic number crunching; this will aid you in deciding if quitting your day job is financially feasible. How much money do you need to live on? How much money would you have to make in order to meet your financial obligations?

- Last of all I want you to know your personality…can you enjoy working alone without any staff or co-workers to support you? If you know that this will be difficult, establish a network of people that are associated with jewelry designing. This could be people you've taken classes with or met at jewelry trade shows, bead society meetings, or at craft shows. There are also forums like About.com for sharing ideas and chatting about jewelry making. (Their Web site is listed on our resource pages).

MAKING YOUR JEWELRY

Being objective can be difficult, especially if it's something you've created. However, don't let your ego get in the way of the creative process or in the way of you making money.

Before you begin to make your jewelry…yes even before you've picked up your first bead, you should analyze the current market. Doing so can definitely make the difference between success and failure. Kicking off your enterprise at the wrong time can be disastrous. Remember several years back when there was a minimalist look in jewelry? Celebrities and magazines were showing either no jewelry or simple creations like the Y necklace. Starting a jewelry line then would have been a date with disaster. Do some R&D (research and development); find out what's selling, and who's selling it. Find out how much they are selling it for and how and where they are selling it…is it someplace where you can sell your items?

I want you to become a jewelry detective and analyze how pieces are constructed. Are they soldered or glued? Did they use precious or base metal findings? What type of stringing material did they use? If they used beads, are they glass, gemstone, acrylic or any combination thereof. Pay close attention to what shapes are used and what colors are combined. Is there a theme or motif associated with the design? I want you to learn to analyze a design from the inside out. If you can handle the jewelry, flip it over and analyze it. I carry a loupe (eyepiece) with me at all times. I know you are supposed to use it for gemstones etc. but I use mine to help me determine how and what materials are used in a jewelry piece. Naturally I only use it when I can do so without arousing suspicion. After a period of time, you will learn how to quickly analyze a piece to determine how much assembly is required. This will give you an idea of how much time they put into making the piece. Make a note on how trendy as opposed to traditional the item is. Use a notebook to document all your information. Be sure to include dates and as much detailed information as you can. My notebook is filled with pictures and info from boutiques and pictures I've downloaded from the Internet or clipped from magazines.

Trust me when I say that taking time to do R& D will reward you by saving you money, time, and frustration.

HOW TO MAKE YOUR JEWELRY BUSINESS A SUCCESS:

1. Analyze the current style of jewelry that's on the market. Pay close attention to the design styles. Again, please don't let your ego stand in the way when you compare your designs to theirs. Ask yourself these questions: How are your designs different? Why would someone choose your jewelry over your competitors?

I want you to work and rework your designs and come up with a style that is truly yours. Don't just buy the same Austrian crystal, attach it to an ear wire, add a rondell and say you have a new creation. Sorry, probably thirty women also created your same earring. Let your creative energy flow by combining different elements from various sources, naturals with synthetics, castings with stampings, ethnic beads with crystals. If you use beads in your designs, search for the unusual or combine them with unusual bead caps. If

10

your designs consist of wire-wrapping, experiment with unusual objects to wrap. Make your color combinations exciting while keeping in mind what they will ultimately be worn with. If you haven't already, invest in a color wheel and use this to help make your color choices exciting. For some reason combining colors still challenges me so I've collected fabric swatches that I use to aide me. They help me when I'm stuck trying to come up with good color combinations. Remember you can't critique yourself enough. I want you to actually write in your notebook why you think your designs are special. This can serve a dual purpose. You can use it when calling on stores and it can help you keep focused on why someone should carry your jewelry instead of your competitor's.

2. I want you to look through current magazines and clothing catalogs. Tear out the pages that have jewelry that appeals to you and add this to your notebook and call it your portfolio of inspiration.

3. I want you to visit trendy clothing stores, making notes in your head on what style of clothing is in and what kind of jewelry is on display.

4. I want you to cruise the Internet and browse through Web sites of fashionable clothes and jewelry. Keep an eye on coming trends, so you will know ahead of time if plaids, stripes, or neon colors will be what fashion dictates. (See our resource page for a link that can help guide you with fashion predictions). Allowing yourself to design jewelry items that follow a hot fashion trend can be exciting; however, proceed with caution. Never ever gear your whole line on a fad, because when it comes and goes, as all fads do, so will your line. Of course, if you plan to create a fad or ride the waves of one, purely for money making purposes, that's ok too, as long as you recognize that its merely temporary. Remember when following the trend, make sure you are on the beginning phase of the fade so that you can ride it for it's duration, otherwise you might find yourself with dated materials that you might not be able to use on other projects.

5. I want you to make notes on styles you see over and over…more than likely they are classic styles and a quarter of your line should be comprised of classics. Utilizing pearls and crystals can definitely help you create classic, timeless pieces.

6. I want you to browse through Italian and French versions of the top fashion magazines. Usually Europeans are ahead of trends and jewelry in these magazines is more daring, exciting and over the top in terms of design and style. Clip some of the pictures that appeal to you and put them in your inspiration portfolio.

7. I want you to go to yard sales, resale or secondhand stores, or antique markets with your detective shield on to investigate how some of the past costume jewelry was constructed. Analyze the combination of colors, the component parts used and how the pieces are combined. Make a note on what period the pieces were made in.

8. Become familiar with designers like Coro, Ciner, Erte and Haskell to name a few. Analyze their style, including what materials they used and how they put them together. Determine what you think makes the pieces so special. Compare your conclusions with your own designs. In what ways are they different…how are they alike? Most of these designers have been highly sought after for years so they are worth studying in detail. I studied Haskell's jewelry and used her designs as inspiration for my line and she is still one of my all-time favorite designers.

9. I want you to learn how to dissect a piece from the bottom up. If you use this technique often, over time you can actually learn to analyze pieces and become very good at determining how it was constructed and what materials were used. This process can help you become a better designer, by using pieces you see as inspiration or future renditions of your own creations.

10. I want you to visit your local hardware store and view it from a jewelry perspective. Instead of just seeing nuts and bolts, look at them from a design standpoint. Think of combining them with jewelry chain or using them in some unique way. Experiment by having them plated in silver, gold, copper, pewter or by using one of the many patina colors. There are also enameling services that can enamel and colorize almost anything, Utilizing this service can give your unique parts a burst of color. I want you to open your mind and substitute traditional for non-traditional. In one of my most successful designs I combined leather beads with crystal, this unconventional way of combining materials worked well and resulted in a best seller for my line.

11. In making the final decision on what kind of jewelry to make, remember there are many options open to you. You could create a line that fills a particular niche, like religious jewelry or school spirit jewelry using school colors and school mascot charms. You could also make jewelry for college gift shops or sororities or you could zero in on metaphysical jewelry. These are just suggestions on ways to create jewelry for a special niche market.

12. I want you to make the jewelry your customers want to buy, which may not necessarily be what you may want to make. Designing only what you like will make your range too limited. Pushing the limits of your creativity can be hard, because it's a battle of artist (that's you) against making jewelry someone wants to buy (your potential customer). Making this important transition is when you change ranks from being a hobbyist to being a professional designer.

I want you to study, read and explore your craft and then with patience and persistence, pursue your passion. Taking time to determine how you want to create, instead of just diving in, will allow you to find out what your particular style of jewelry should be. I know that if you open your mind, you too can create pieces that are uniquely you. Whatever decisions you make on the direction you want your jewelry to take, remember, don't be afraid to experiment, and let your true design senses explode with new possibilities.

EXPAND YOUR CREATIVITY WITH TOOLS AND TIPS OF THE TRADE

I want you to learn to use basic tools of the trade with ease and flair. One tool that can open a whole world of creative freedom is the rotary tool (trade name Dremel). They come with several interchangeable attachments. Once you have mastered using this tool, you can drill, sand, pierce and alter almost any jewelry part. When using this tool, always use it in conjunction with a drill press adapter or a vise designed for rotary tools. These handy gadgets will hold your items firmly to avoid fingers being pricked or worst yet jabbed. If you work with glass or stone beads and want to enlarge holes, you can use this tool with a diamond bit. If you need tons of glass/stone beads drilled, invest in a flex shaft. A flex shaft is pencil sized and is more comfortable to use for extended periods. It will also allow you to use it in water, which is necessary when drilling glass.

I want you to learn how to solder. Basic soldering tools can be purchased from your local bead store or online. By soldering metal parts together you can alter components, creating totally original pieces. Your local library, bookstore or online sources should have detailed instruction books and information on the subject. If you happen to live in a metropolitan area, you can find classes at bead stores. Another tool that is indispensable for designers is a micrometer. If you don't already own one, get one. It is inexpensive and a "must-have" for any designer. It will measure your beads and findings in millimeters, so that you won't have to guess the sizes of your parts. Besides when reordering your products you can give your supplier exact sizes. Having this handy tool can give you a professional edge when you require beads or components that are a certain size.

TIPS TO A BETTER JEWELRY LINE

1) Make sure your work is durable and will hold up. Wear any new design that has a new method of construction. Doing so can eliminate potential flaws and avoid embarrassing returns.

2) Make sure you are using the best materials to construct your jewelry. Never use a glue gun to construct any part of your designs. This includes, but is not limited to, putting on posts or gluing what you may consider the smallest attachment. Glue guns or hot glue will not hold up. Pieces attached this way will pop off clean, leaving no visible signs of glue. Most accessory imports are made this way and perhaps this is the reason they have a reputation for falling apart.

3) Make sure your endings and the back of your jewelry is just as attractive as the front. Double check wherever jump rings connect, make sure they are firmly closed; this is where your soldering skills can help. If you are making earrings and they are slightly on the heavy side or the sections swing and twist a lot, use a heavier gauge jump ring. If you wire or rosary wrap your jewelry, make sure the ends of the wire are securely tucked so they don't scratch or irritate. A great tool to aid in rounding the ends of your wire is a cup bur. You should be able to find this handy tool at your local bead store.

4) I do want you to make custom metal tags for your jewelry, ones that identify you as the designer. These tags can be made of base metal or precious metals, like sterling silver or gold, (visit our resource pages for links). You should also make small printed labels on your computer that completely describe what you are using in your creations, i.e. gold-filled items, vintage beads, semi-precious stones, etc. Doing this is educational for your customers and your stores. I've found that many store owners and their employees need educating on what they are selling; don't assume they know the quality of the items you use. Good

accurate detailed information will help to explain why you need a certain amount of money for your jewelry. Remember when it comes to selling your items you can't provide too much information, informing the potential customer is very important and detailed personalized labels will definitely help.

5) I do want you to think about branding your jewelry. You've heard a lot about branding and large corporations, but think of this in terms of your line. Branding simply means giving an identity to your line..it means your style, or the message you want to convey with your jewelry. Come up with something you add or do to all your pieces to give them your own special stamp. You might choose a tiny charm to add to each piece of your jewelry and carry the theme out in your bags or wrapping paper. I have a friend who uses little miniature dragon charms that she attaches to almost all her jewelry. She even hand stamps her wrapping paper, bags, and business cards with dragons. So come up with your own unique identity for your jewelry. It's a special touch and something that can help you brand your jewelry.

6) Make a commitment to stay creative and fresh for your repeat customers, doing so will guarantee you future business.

7) Keep creative channels open by learning all you can about jewelry making. Take classes and study online to learn new techniques and to perfect your personal style.

NOW THAT YOU KNOW WHAT KIND OF JEWELRY YOU WANT TO CREATE

Refresh yourself on the finer points of getting your product ready to market. One major decision you will have to decide on is should you make expensive or inexpensive jewelry ($30 to $300 retail). Evaluate your items to see where they fall price-wise. Keep in mind, the higher your price point, the more you will have to work at building your image to demand your price.

Making jewelry that requires the use of sterling silver, karat gold, crystal, or lamp work beads, would fall into this category. Choosing the method to sell your line is important in maintaining your image too, so you will have to do more homework to make sure you choose the right representation or the right boutiques. You wouldn't try to sell a high-end item at a flea market or a low-end clothing store. A more expensive line will require more monetary expenditure for start-up material costs. Your potential boutique clients and department stores may also put more demands on you to provide repairs, and will definitely demand that your items be almost perfect in construction and design.

With jewelry that is less expensive, you probably won't have to concern yourself with repairs, since customers don't consider it a major investment. Your costs are usually less, and repairs seldom. Customers usually dispose of defective inexpensive jewelry. If you choose this market, keep in mind that it is highly competitive since it is saturated with imports. The import market for jewelry and accessories in this country has truly affected the cottage accessory business. The most obvious reason is that labor and production expenses are much cheaper in foreign countries. The small designer and manufacturer in the United States have an almost impossible position in this market, since having competitive prices is difficult. We will address the import issue in a later chapter.

Choosing mid-to high-mid-range jewelry would probably be a wise choice, since your designs and prices could range from high-low to high-medium. This of course, is a personal decision but an important one that you should consider carefully.

ഐക്കൊഐക്കൊഐക്കൊഐക്കൊഐക്കൊ

Inspirational Quote: "To realize what is possible, you have to see the invisible!"

CHAPTER 2

WHICH WILL IT BE: ONE-OF-A-KIND OR PRODUCTION JEWELRY

ONE-OF-A-KIND JEWELRY

Every jewelry artist wants something different, so deciding which road your jewelry business will travel is entirely up to you. If you create one-of-a-kind pieces, you will usually be making them on speculation as opposed to having pre-determined orders. Your hope is that someone will purchase them from you at a later date by whatever method you choose to sell. There are some advantages to creating a one-of-a-kind line, from an artistic standpoint; you won't get bored with producing the same design over and over. This is the primary reason most artists like doing one of a kind. Another major advantage of a one-of-a-kind line is materials; you'll be able to buy small amounts of inventory. You can take advantage of special items in limited supply. A unique string of gemstones or a few special vintage beads can easily be utilized in your designs. Because you can invest less in inventory, you can afford to buy more unique items.

Having stated some advantages of a one-of-a-kind line, there are some disadvantages. One major one is that you will find it difficult, if not impossible to get an accurate estimate of the time needed to create your items. Because you are creating and assembling the piece as you go, separating the two can be difficult, but you will still need to have some idea of the time spent in making the piece. Invest in a good stopwatch. Each time you sit down at your design table, clock in. If you have to get up for any reason, remember to clock out. This is extremely important. Keep a notebook and pen nearby. Realistically, you really can't expect your designs to pay for your ponder and experimentation time, keeping track of how much time you spend on each piece can be used as a rough guide for determining the final selling price of your items, along with whatever materials you use.

If you decide to create one-of-a-kind jewelry, your items will usually be sold in small boutiques. Oftentimes, they use the one-of-a-kind aspect as a selling point to customers who prefer originality, limited quantities and a more personal relationship with the artist. Larger department stores are usually not interested in one-of-kind-lines. They prefer production lines. There are some chain stores that have departments within the jewelry department that specialize in one-of-a-kind jewelry. To find out what department stores carry handcrafted items, you will have to fish around. If you have visited the store and noticed handcrafted jewelry, ask someone in that department; they might know how you can get in touch with the buyer. If you haven't visited the store, telephone them and ask for management in the jewelry department.

More than likely with a one-of-a-kind line you will be making all the jewelry yourself. That's okay, just don't overestimate the amount you can produce in the time allowed. Remember, you will have interruptions with sales and administrative duties that will definitely cut into your design time.

PRODUCTION JEWELRY

Developing a production line can mean duplicating your design a few times with limited editions or duplicating the design multiple times as long as it sells. A primary component of achieving sales is perfecting how efficient your production process is.

Mass-producing jewelry, even on a small scale, requires a different mindset, and like one-of-a-kind designing, mass-production has plenty of advantages and disadvantages. Let's start with the disadvantages. The most obvious is the loss of creativity. The routine and repetitive nature of duplicating the same piece over and over can be boring to some designers. Personally, I like the idea of not having to be on a creative roll every day.

Another disadvantage of production designing is that you will have to avoid one-of-a-kind materials, such as unusual gemstones or other materials that may not be available in quantity. Oftentimes I'd find the perfect stone or findings, but because it was impossible to get easily or because it was a unique material, I'd have to abandon it for something that was less creative but attainable. Before I commit to a finding, stone or bead, I always ask the supplier about the availability of the piece. For example, if I thought a supplier or an item would present a problem, I would purchase all of the items from them at one time. I had an agreement with a bead store in which I would liquidate my outdated, unused items at half the price that I paid. This allowed me to turn my money over and helped with my cash flow.

Because production designing has more of a limited price range, you will be forced to limit your use of expensive materials and learn how to find adequate substitutions. Learning how and when to substitute is important. Remember, shaving off even a few cents from an item you use can affect your bottom line. Production jewelry will also force you to streamline your designs. You simply won't have the luxury of being able to include time-consuming details. With experience you will learn to recognize what you can do and what you can't do. Every time you design a new piece, think about how leaving out a particular step would affect the salability or functionality of it. In production work, the detail and intricacy of your work will be limited.

Finally, a major disadvantage is that mass-producing jewelry under a wholesale deadline can be stressful. With major department stores, deadlines are strictly enforced; being even one day late can cost you the account. At this point you might ask, "Why would anyone want to mass-produce the same pieces of jewelry over and over, working under a deadline?" You may be thinking that that's not why you want to become a jewelry artist. Remember the flip side of this is creating one-of-a-kind pieces on speculation that someone may or may not decide to purchase from you. Also consider that you will be getting inventory ready for shows that may or may not have good attendance or earn you much profit. Therefore, production and one of a kind designing are equally valid ways of making a living from your craft.

ADVANTAGES OF A PRODUCTION LINE

One major advantage is money. Many artists prefer knowing that the pieces they make are sold before they make them. Working this way can give you a sense of security, especially if you need a reliable income and making jewelry is your primary source of earning a living. The ability to produce multiples of your pieces could make the difference between making a living as an artist or needing a day job. Having a good, reliable income rolling in from your wholesale accounts can be a great form of self-employment and a wonderful incentive.

Production affords you the ability to work assembly-line fashion on a dozen or more of the same pieces at the same time. Doing so will enable you to complete several of the same items much faster than if you made them one at a time, from start to finish. When mass-producing your jewelry, streamlining each production step is vital for managing your time. For example, if your design can use a ready-made clasp, carefully consider if it's worth the extra time you would have to take to make handcrafted ones. Eliminating even a few seconds from each step of making the design can knock hours off a full-scale production run. In production, it's simply not efficient to include time-consuming details that don't affect the salability of the piece. You should design your line with production in mind and always try to design pieces that will assemble and produce easily. When you do production work, remember everything is exaggerated. If there is a problem area with a piece, try imagining the problem if you had to produce five hundred pieces. Revising and redesigning pieces that you have to spend too much time on will become part of your daily ritual. Pieces that take too much time or are tedious to produce will affect your bank account if you include them in your line.

Another advantage of production is that making a great design and reproducing it lots of times will spread the cost over all your pieces. In short you can make more money by spreading the design cost over the entire production of the piece. Single one-of-a-kind pieces that you design will naturally have higher price points to compensate for the time spent designing the piece.

Although I talked about creativity in production as a disadvantage for most artists, I find the lack of creativity to be an advantage because I like the repetitive nature of producing the same item. Listening to good music or a great audio book actually makes this type of work pleasurable. Besides having to be consistently creative and original can be a different form of stress.

SUMMING IT ALL UP

Production jewelry will definitely force you to become efficient with your time, since most of your orders will have delivery deadlines. By getting to know your suppliers you will know how much lead time you need for delivery of the items you need in your orders. You will also learn how to predict with accuracy how much production time you will need to assemble them. Figuring out these major points will give you a realistic turnaround time or delivery date. *Major point:* Increase whatever time you think you need to produce an order by at least 25%. If you think you will need four days to produce an order, make your ship/delivery date five days. Learn from my experience, this additional time will more than likely be used for unexpected emergencies.

As you can see, production and one-of-a-kind jewelry-making both have their pluses and minuses. A good friend of mine has the best of both worlds. She makes one of a kind jewelry that she retails throughout the country, and from those pieces she chooses which ones she will put into her production line. She chooses them based on their sales and how easy they are to assemble, then wholesales them to several major store accounts.

22

You should think long and hard before you make a final decision on how you want to structure your business from a design standpoint. Every artist wants something different from his or her craft. Some want the creative freedom to design whatever they can imagine, regardless of whether they can sell it or not, while others want to somehow blend some creative freedom with some business savvy to supplement their income. Still there are others who want to turn their craft into a business to earn a living. Whether you choose production or one-of-a-kind jewelry, creating something you love and selling it can give you a natural high.

THINGS TO REMEMBER

1. You will have to streamline the cost of your supplies for your wholesale jewelry pieces. Shaving even a few cents off the cost of them can net you hundreds of dollars in extra profits a year.

2. Each step in the production process is vital for managing your time. If your design can use a ready-made charm instead of the hand-hammered one that takes you 10 minutes to fabricate, think long and hard about whether the hand-hammered one is necessary. Remember eliminating minutes can knock hours off a production order.

3. You should set up your workspace for efficiency and volume production. You'll also need extra space to store large quantities of unused materials and to store your finished jewelry before shipping.

4. You may need duplicate sets of some of your tools and supplies, enough for helpers to create several copies of the same design simultaneously.

5. The single most important thing to remember for production work is that when purchasing your component parts, make sure they can be purchased repeatedly with no problem. Purchase parts from suppliers who can guarantee you deliveries of the pieces you use. With my line, I try to use components that more than one supplier carries. Of course this is not always possible. Often times I have to take a chance on the availability of a bead or component if it is unique or different, then try to judge when to pull the items from my line. Needless to say, on several occasions my judgment has been inaccurate and I've had to improvise as best I could to ship an order. One funny incidence occurred when I got an order for 600 pair of earrings from Cache, which at the time had 200 stores. The earrings were made using some brown Picasso beads. Because I hadn't anticipated getting such a large order, I had only purchased enough to make approximately 200 pairs. After a grueling, nonproductive search to find "THE BEAD," I finally concluded that it was like finding a needle in a haystack. I found the shape but the color was light blue, with no Picasso variations on it. As my deadline neared, I gave up and purchased the light blue beads. Using some etchall, which is a non-acid that mattes glass I matted each and every one of them. I purchased some brown water-based acrylic spray paint and proceeded to paint each bead and blotched them with a sea sponge soaked in a darker brown paint. I baked them in my home oven on a low temperature. I worked on those beads for over three days before I had enough pieces to make the earrings. Tired, but undefeated, I shipped the order right on the deadline. Actually they turned out to be more beautiful than the originals, but producing the beads and turning them into earrings under pressure was something I never want to do again and it was a lesson well learned. That's why if you choose to do production, always "over-buy." It's better than under-buying. There were times when I'd be convinced that a particular design would be a "mega-seller," but instead I ended up selling average quantities, so I would end up with extra inventory. Remember, with production, extra inventory is something that you will accumulate. However, if you buy at good prices and find a source to buy back some of your items when you no longer need them, in the end your balance sheet should work to your advantage.

6. In order to protect your business, you should establish a business relationship with back-up suppliers by giving them regular orders throughout the year so that they will have an incentive to accommodate you in a pinch.

7. Employees – If you do production work you will definitely need help, so make sure you incorporate the expense of employees into your jewelry prices. If you are use to working solo, having employees will take getting use to. Managing and overseeing them will definitely take a large percentage of your time, so having projects or things that you need to accomplish can be rather trying. With my line, I spend the first part of my day dealing with employees and reserve afternoons for things that I need to do independently.

Inspirational Quote: "Nothing can stop the man with the right mental attitude from achieving his goal; nothing on earth can help the man with the wrong mental attitude," Thomas Jefferson.

CHAPTER 3

HOW TO PRICE YOUR JEWELRY

Determining a fair price for your jewelry means you will have to separate yourself from any emotional attachments and view each item using a simple equation: labor + workspace costs + materials + profit = fair price.

How do you come up with a fair price? That's the question I'm most often asked in my marketing classes. How much should I sell my pieces for? I wish I could answer this in a sentence or two, but there are so many things to consider, such as how much is your time worth? What are your material costs? Should you add in something for the rent, the tools you use, the paper towels and the light bulbs? How much time did you spend getting supplies, packaging, shipping or delivering them? Should you also add in these items? The answer to all of the questions above is "yes", in caps... **YES!** If you don't include everything involved in making your pieces, you will not make money. I'm assuming you are reading this book to turn your passion and love for jewelry-making into dollars. So, yes again, you will have to cover all of your expenses and I mean all of them or you will not reap any financial rewards...no "dinero," it's as simple as that.

A general rule of thumb in pricing your jewelry is to mark up your total cost three times for retail and two times for wholesale. Remember this rule is only general, because again there are lots of variables.

Pricing your items can be confusing. You don't want to price them so high that nobody will buy them, but you don't want to price them so low that you don't make any money.

Understanding the process of selling will help you price your items. Retail is the ultimate end of the selling process. Wholesale is when your jewelry will change hands or ownership before retail. Tax is not added to the wholesale price. Manufacturers (people who make products, that's you), sell to wholesalers who sell to retail stores who in turn, sell to the consumer. If you are retailing your own items you will have a distinct advantage and should be able to make more profit minus whatever expenses you incur in selling your items, this includes show fees, advertising...etc. At each step of the manufacturing level, items become more expensive. Each successive step adds its cost and profit to the original cost of the item.

If you plan to wholesale your jewelry (sell to retail stores, galleries or through a rep) you will want to price them as cheaply as possible without jeopardizing the integrity of your product. Remember, with wholesaling you have to leave room for the end seller to make a profit.

When you think you've reached a selling price, do some comparison-shopping and compare your prices to similar retail items. Do you want your price to be higher or lower? There are no firm rules about how you set your prices, but you should keep your ultimate goal in mind, selling your product and making a profit.

WHAT WILL THE MARKET BEAR?

You should definitely keep in mind what the market will tolerate when setting your prices. Remember to pay attention to every minute detail. You will need to make sure you are comparing similar items in terms of materials used and the construction method. If you haven't already, please do your homework by checking out stores and magazines, noting the price of items similar to yours. This is an important step to complete and should be ongoing to stay current. Make an excel file/spreadsheet to place this information in; this file will come in handy when determining your prices. I named my file/spreadsheet "MARKET BEAR SHEET." You will find that some of your designs can be marked up more than the standard mark-up and some can be marked up less.

With experience, you will be able to eyeball your pieces after accounting for the materials used and the time it took to make them to determine the highest selling price. Speaking of materials used, I also have a 'MARKET BEAR MATERIAL SHEET". This sheet is used to update any materials I use in my designs, like the stock metals market for gold and sterling silver items. The daily market price of precious metals can change with each order I make which changes my bottom line. So keeping this sheet updated is crucial. I also update my "Market Bear" sheet whenever I change suppliers, whether it's to get a better-quality item or a better price point.

Another tip on pricing is to not let one-time deals affect your selling prices. Let's say you've found a closeout deal on sterling silver and this find can positively affect your selling price. Use this special price to make more profit on your items; don't lower your selling price because you scored on a one-time deal.

I can't stress enough that I want you to make items that will give you a good profit for the supplies and the design time you put into them. Usually this includes making lots of compromises. You may want to use all gold-filled findings, but if your price points will suffer, substitute. Use a combination of gold-filled and vermeil so that your info tag can still say that you've used some gold-filled. You may want to use all sterling, but if your price points will suffer, use a combination of sterling and pewter. Pewter has the advantage of wearing well and will not rub off like silver-plated base metals. There are some items in my designs that don't lend themselves to the cheapest price. These items include ear wires, clasps, crimps and stringing materials. I call these items my foundation items. Using the best-quality items for your foundation will pay off if you want to create jewelry that will last and hold-up well. Aside from my foundation items, I try to spend my money where it counts, where my potential buyer can easily see the difference.

28

We can't end this segment without spending some time addressing Chinese imports and their effect on your line. The globalization of America has indeed affected how and what we consume and the costume-jewelry industry has not been spared. Some insiders call this the "Wal-Mart-ization" of the jewelry industry. While this is considered bad from one perspective, from another it may actually drive up the value of handcrafted items. Unless you've had your head stuck in an oven, you've noticed all the cheap imported jewelry not only at Wal-Mart but at flea markets and shopping malls. You can easily recognize them because of the price and the cheap component parts used to make them. Trust me when I say that there are ways you can compete with imports and win:

- Use the best components you can. Sterling silver and gold-filled items will increase your customers' perceived value of your jewelry.

- If you use beads in your line, make sure you use good-quality beads. The glass should be clear and the holes clean, smooth and well-reamed. Sometimes I'll use Indian beads, which may be of lesser quality, if I want my piece to have more of an ethnic flavor.

- When given the opportunity, have some imported jewelry next to some of the items you've created. Using good materials and good construction, along with great design, will win customers over every time. It's very easy to recognize the difference when they are side by side.

- You can offer your customers an education about the value of what you've designed. Personal contact with your buyer is important. Keep in mind that there are a large number of buyers who want well-made, quality items. In this mass-produced, cookie-cutter world, it is extremely important to some people to not only have good-quality handmade items, but to have a relationship with the people who make them.

My conclusions about imports and competing with them is make the best jewelry you can, and sell your pieces at fair prices. Quality and well-thought-out designs will take you to the bank.

CALCULATING YOUR PRICE POINTS

Don't let the process of setting your prices be confusing or complicated. Remember, pricing your items boils down to just one thing, setting a marketable price that covers what you spend (expenses) and paying yourself.

All businesses have two basic types of costs (or expenses), fixed costs and variable costs. These two costs added together will determine your operating expenses and let you arrive at price points that are profitable for you.

FIXED COSTS

Fixed costs are the costs that don't change. These include things like your rent, licenses and any long-term loan payments. These costs will remain relatively stable even when your sales don't. If you produce 20 necklaces a day for your line, or you produce 30, your rent will stay the same. Fixed costs can usually be estimated at the beginning of the year and projected over the next 12 months. Other fixed costs might include accounting, administrative fees and marketing expenses, such as advertising and trade show fees.

VARIABLE COSTS

Variable costs simply mean any costs in your line that changes. Your variable costs can rise and fall, depending on how many necklaces you produce, what materials you use, labor (remember to pay yourself as if you had an employee), and even your shipping costs. A good example of a variable cost is that you might need 10 feet of sterling chain to produce 20 necklaces but if you produce 30 necklaces you will need 15 feet of sterling chain. So your cost will vary depending on your production level. A 20-oz bottle of glue may produce 50 of a particular item and 100 of another, so you will have to use approximations to determine the glue costs for each. As your production volume goes up, so will your variable costs. You can estimate variable costs at the beginning of the year, but remember they are merely estimates. Variable costs not only include the cost of the materials used in your line but they can also include certain utilities, classes, and any related business expenses that might be affected by the amount of production. Remember to keep your receipts, they will help you to get maximum tax deductions at the end of the year and they will keep your accountant very happy. These expenses are to be added up and spread out over your overall sales. Since my business has been in existence for years, I am able to estimate my variables fairly accurately and incorporate a percentage amount into the final asking price of my jewelry.

CROSS OVERS ON FIXED AND VARIABLE EXPENSES

It is impossible to foresee all of your costs; did you remember business insurance? Adding on a 10 percent contingency to both your fixed and variable costs is a wise precaution.

Labor is one category that will usually have to be split between the above categories. The salary you pay your assistant for production work is called direct labor and is a variable cost because what you pay out will depend on how many items they produce. Labor costs to your bookkeeper or accountant are fixed expenses because their salaries will remain the same regardless of how much or how little you produce.

Utilities are another cost that is split between fixed and variable. Your phone bill for instance, probably won't change much whether your production increases or decreases. On the other hand keeping your studio lights on longer because you're working more hours will cause your electric bill to vary.

Cost of materials should be included in your variable expenses, because, like your labor, these expenses will rise and fall depending on your production. They can also vary between fixed and variable because you might have some items you use in every piece of jewelry you produce and because you always buy it at the same cost, the cost of that item may be fixed. A good example of this would be if you use beading wire for all your necklaces and the price doesn't fluctuate. By writing down exactly what you use in your line, you should easily be able to determine what your variable, fixed or cross-over expenses are.

DETERMINING YOUR LABOR COSTS

Without Employees

Many inexperienced or beginning designers exclude labor in the cost of their products because they do not have employees or helpers assembling their jewelry. Just because you are a solo designer doesn't mean that you shouldn't pay yourself and more than likely you will grow and add employees. Do some soul searching and come up with a realistic hourly rate. Don't be ridiculous and come up with some unobtainable amount that you know you won't be able to pay yourself. On the other hand, don't undervalue your time just because you're doing something you love doing. Besides being good to yourself, another prime reason you should pay yourself is because when your business grows and you have employees, you won't have to change your prices to existing clients. Having incorporated your labor costs into your final prices will keep your prices stable.

With Employees

You must decide how much your employees will be paid per hour to produce your items. If you have done a good job of timing yourself with the original samples, when you give the piece to an employee to make, you should have a fairly accurate accounting of how much time it will take. Because I am usually faster and have timed my pieces several times, I add about 20% to 25% more time to each item, in fairness to my employees. Although you are paying by the hour, you must have some method in place that will allow you to arrive at a fair employee wage and one that is profitable for you.

For example, if an item takes you 15 minutes and you want to add 20% more time for your employees, the total time to assemble the item would be 18 minutes. If your rate of pay is $10 per hour, you would divide $10 by 60 minutes (1 hour) which will give you approximately 0.17 cents per minute times 18 minutes assembly time, the approximate price you would pay to assemble the item would be $3.06. Therefore, if your employee only gives you three items per hour, you are receiving $9.18 ($3.06 times 3 for a total of $9.18) per hour of production work from your employee and you are losing eighty-two cents every hour or $6.56 per eight-hour day or $1705.60 per year, per employee. Having these numbers in place before you hire an employee will allow you to know approximately how much production you should receive from an employee even though you are paying them by the hour.

I keep an Excel spreadsheet to keep tabs on my employee costs per week. If you pay your employees $10 per hour and they work 20 hours per week the weekly cost of labor would be $200.

The second step in figuring out your costs will be to determine the total cost of supplies needed to make one finished item. Make sure you include everything associated with the item. Include glues, headpins, wire, beads, crimps and anything, no matter how small in this supply total. Included on our sample forms pages is an example of a labor and materials workup sheet. To download a PDF blank form visit our Web site.

Next, you should determine how many finished items one person could produce in a week. This will be extremely important if you are working with a major department store. Your purchase order, or "P.O." as it is commonly called in the industry, will always have a firm due-date. So getting an accurate estimate of the time needed for each worker to finish an item is extremely important. Armed with this information, you will also be able to determine if you need additional help or overtime hours to meet your deadline. Be realistic. Don't think that you can do it all yourself, if you know going into it that you'll have to stretch. Keep in mind the point we made earlier regarding increasing the estimated production time by at least 20%. Sometimes this is possible, sometimes not, but any amount of time you can add over what you think you will need, will help. Remember to always work ahead of your deadline to avoid last-minute stress and maintain good quality control.

After determining your labor and supply costs, you will need to multiply the cost of supplies-per-item by the number of products produced in a week. For example if the cost of materials per item is $2 and you can produce 100 items a week, the amount added would be $200. Add this figure to your weekly labor costs.

The items above would be $200(Labor) + $200(cost of supplies) = $400

Divide this figure by the number of products produced in a week (So $400 labor/materials divided by 100 finished products a week would be $4 per item).

If you will be wholesaling your products, multiply this number by 2 to 2½, which would give you a wholesale price of $10 per item at 2½.

Armed with your figures, compare your cost to similar products on the retail market. If your price is more than similar jewelry, you may need to reduce it by substituting less expensive materials, cutting your per hour or per piece price, or by finding a time-saving way to decrease your production time. If your price is significantly less than similar products, you may want to consider raising your price. If your items will allow it, you can triple them so that a $4 item will wholesale for $12. There are no hard and set rules.

When setting your wholesale prices, remember your retailer will have to double or triple your price to make a profit. A standard markup for a retail store is to double the cost of items. This is called keystone, a keystone markup is a markup that is equal to the cost of the item they are purchasing, essentially taking the cost of an item and doubling it to determine the retail price. Retail stores have used keystone markup for decades. If there is room in your price to allow your boutique or retailer to do more than keystone, you or your representatives can use this as a selling point to acquire new accounts. The more profit a retailer can make, the more they will want to purchase your items.

If you are selling your jewelry directly to the public (this could be online, at a craft fair, a house party, etc.), you will be selling at retail. You should multiply the cost of your expenses by three to get the retail price. The three-times mark-up should cover any additional expenses (show fees, booth rentals, etc.) involved in retailing your own jewelry.

Remember that the wholesale price is the price you charge when you sell your jewelry to a retailer (the person who sells the jewelry to the public).

FYI: Too often designers price their items at retail when they are starting out, with no idea of how to price them at wholesale. Remember stores double the wholesale price to set the retail price they will charge customers. (For example, if a store pays $30 for an item, they will need to mark that item up to a minimum of $60.

SIMPLE FORMULA EXAMPLE:	
Cost of item (this includes labor and parts)	$10
Wholesale Price	$20 to $25
With rep's fee @ 20%, (add to final wholesale or retail price)	$4 to $5
Retail Price	$48 to $60

In the simple formula example, an item that costs $10 to produce, including labor and parts, should wholesale for $20 to $25. If you have professional representation you should add the rep's commission (20% of the wholesale total), making the new wholesale price of the item $24 to $30 Keep in mind that the retail store will double and/or triple that figure for a final price of $48 to $60. It's now easy to see why price points are so important to you and to the retailer.

TRACKING YOUR INCOME

Since your aim is to be self-employed, your income is called profit. Income is when you actually get paid, not when you make the product you are going to sell. There is a huge array of software on the market to help you keep track of your income, but I prefer to use Microsoft Excel spreadsheets. With a little help from an Excel book, or the help menu included in the Excel program, you should be able to set up a spreadsheet to record all sales and incoming monies received. Just keep in mind that your total is only what you earned. It is simply income or what you have coming in. To figure out what you actually put in your pocket you will have to subtract what is going out. The formula for figuring out what you actually earned or profited is "INCOME – COST = PROFIT."

THE BOTTOM LINE

Profit is what is left over after subtracting variable and fixed costs from your sales. Naturally, to make a profit, you must be able to sell your jewelry for more than the cost to make it and you must be able to sell it for a price high enough to cover both the variable and fixed costs associated with making it.

THINGS TO REMEMBER WHEN PRICING YOUR JEWELRY

1. When designing new pieces, keep your price points in focus at all times. This simply means that every single item, no matter how small, must be used in your final computations. Let inspiration and price be primary when you shop for new components for a future design. Keeping good records and prices will help you to bring your final designs in at fair prices and provide enough profit for you and your buyers, whether they are wholesale or retail. (Visit our resource pages for a great link to a Web site that provides a free jewelry-pricing calculator).

2. Remember, if you have representation for your line, you must add the rep's fee to the final wholesale cost. Use a "mark-up" calculator for this. A mark-up calculator is a calculator that has a mark-up key. The reason for using this particular calculator when determining your commission fees will become obvious with the following example. Let's assume you want to add a 15% rep's commission to a $25 bracelet. On most calculators $25 times 15% equals $3.75 for a total price of $28.75. Now assume it's time to pay your rep and you want to deduct the 15% commission fee your rep is due. Multiply $28.75 times 15%, the result is $4.31. You would be overpaying your rep by .56 cents ($4.31-$3.75).

With a mark-up calculator, the original mark-up on $25 would have been $4.41 instead of $3.75. The earrings should have cost $29.41. Now when you deduct 15% to pay your rep, you will not be overpaying. This also means your rep is making more money, since he will receive $4.41 instead of $3.75. This may seem small, but when you have large orders and add your totals over the year, it can add up to a large deficit. Many manufacturers are paying their reps more than they realize, when they use a regular calculator to figure the price of their accessories. Of course this also makes your accessories slightly higher in price. The only way around this problem is to assign a set commission amount for each accessory item and add all the set rates of all the accessories in an order, when it's time to pay your rep. Most reps will not like this method since the fixed-rate method guarantees they get only what you agreed upon and not the slight extra they get by multiplying 15% times the entire order.

3. I like to set my prices, whether retail or wholesale, in round numbers. If my cost for producing an item comes to $20.25, I'll take the price to the next whole number and make it $21, it keeps my bookkeeping easier and simpler.

AT THE END OF THE YEAR

The required paperwork when running any business can be demanding. Just because your business is small, it does not mean that some of the same requirements aren't there. If you feel challenged in this area, hire a bookkeeper that understands your business because tracking sales inventory, determining expenses, collecting and reporting sales taxes can be a little daunting. To avoid making expensive, aggravating and time-consuming mistakes, have a professional set up a bookkeeping system that is tailored just for you.

I have always credited myself in knowing how my business works and yes, that includes the drudgery of paperwork. I believe that in order to delegate responsibility you should know from the ground up all aspects of how your business ticks. The bottom line is that even on your level there will be lots of paperwork, but you can make this daunting task much easier if you take time to isolate and organize during the year. Please take a look at the cost-calculation worksheet in our forms section. If you use the worksheet properly, you can hand it over to your accountant at the end of the year, along with receipts from the year's purchases. Your cost-calculation worksheet will have spaces for your variable and fixed expenses. If you combine these together you will have your operating expenses. At the top of your cost calculation worksheet you will find an area to record your annual depreciation.

More than likely, your annual depreciation will be something you can use to your advantage at tax time. This area should include all your capital expenditures. Capital expenditures will include the expenses you incurred in setting up your business, studio or workshop. This would include the cost of all equipment and tools you purchased to set up your business. For example, if you bought a computer, kilns, torches for soldering and associated equipment and the total cost was $5,000, you should estimate the lifetime use of the equipment. Lifetime use of the equipment simply means how long you can use an item before you need to purchase another one. So if you estimate that to be 10 years, the annual (yearly) depreciation of your equipment would be $500. With this sheet, you would include copies of your original invoices to establish that you did spend the total amount stated on your purchases.

Inspirational quote: "If I only had...I could if...I tried but...how many excuses can you come up with? Every day you make a choice, choose not to use these as reasons why you don't follow your dream," Susie Edwards.

CHAPTER 4

CREATING A ROADMAP: BUSINESS PLAN 101

Before you start your new venture I want you to take some time to prepare a business plan. A business plan is like a roadmap to your desired economic position. If you were taking a trip across country, before you left, would you figure out your route or drive randomly? I'm sure you would map your way and by doing so you would save lots of time, money, energy and aggravation. The same analysis applies to your jewelry business.

Your business plan will help you see where you want to go and how you plan to get there. It will help you clearly define your business and identify your goals. Having a well though-out plan can help you handle unforeseen complications and make good sound business decisions. A large part of the entire business plan lies in the process of you having to research and think about your future business. Writing out your plans in a systematic way forces you to look at your ideas critically, and although this may take some time now, you will avoid costly mistakes later.

There are tons of software, books and Web sites devoted to creating a business plan. They can help you tweak your numbers and make beautiful color graphs and bar charts. These will merely provide you with extra bells and whistles. You can utilize them if you want but you don't need any of them to create a good solid business plan. Remember, your business plan doesn't have to be complicated. If you are trying to get investors to invest in your jewelry company, you will have to make your plan more detailed and the whistles and bells mentioned above will definitely add to your total package. Making your plan as professional as possible will help show potential investors that your business ideas are well thought-out and that you understand what it takes to start and manage a business. If you are seeking investors, you will also need a personal financial, or net worth statement. The primary worry of investors is losing money. You may be in the business of making beautiful jewelry because you love it but investors are in the business of investing to make a profit. So pay attention to the little things in finalizing your business proposal if you are going after private funding. Do your homework; the Internet can provide you with a wealth of information, as can the Small Business Administration (see their Web site URL on our resource pages).

Since getting your business plan on paper is the first step to making it happen, read through our business plan 101 for specifics that will guide you through the fine points. Instead of just talking in abstract ways about what you think your business and profit potential can be, a business plan will allow you to see it clearly, in black and white. Thinking through every aspect of what you hope to accomplish in advance will help you avoid the mistakes made by underestimating important details. Estimating numbers that are as close as you can get to the real deal can give you a plan that mirrors your venture fairly accurately. Remember, making mistakes could cost you not only time but your future business, your life's savings, your job and anything else that you have invested, in order to get your dream going. So let's get started on the actual plan that will transform your life. Your business plan outline should consist of two parts, the master description and the financial data.

BUSINESS PLAN OUTLINE

Part I - Master Description

A. Description of your business

B. Marketing

C. Competition

D. Operating procedures

E. Personnel (if applicable)

F. Summary: include mission statement, goals & objectives

Part II - Financial Data

A. Finances

B. Supply list

C. Budget

D. Balance sheet

E. Break-even analysis

F. Summary

MASTER DESCRIPTION BREAKDOWN

A. Description of business/business overview - In this section includes a brief description of what you plan for your jewelry business. Will you be making vintage, one-of-a-kind or production jewelry? Will you gear your pieces for the junior, teen, baby or adult market? Figuring out your target market, or who your audience will be, should be decided early on. You will need this to determine who you are designing for. Be concise and professional with your descriptions. If you are applying for a loan, this is where you would state how you are going to use the money. You should also include the name and location of your business in this section.

B. Marketing/selling plan - In this section include how and where you plan to sell your jewelry. Include a full description of exactly what your line will look like. This is a big and important part of your business plan. What kind of pricing and promotional strategy will you use? If you've decided that you want to target higher end, small-to middle-size boutiques, this is where you would put that information. If your target is one-of-a-kind art jewelry, this is where you would put what type of galleries you would contact. You should have already decided what sex, age and income level you plan to market to.

In your marketing plan, be as specific as possible; give numbers, sources and any other pertinent information to help you isolate and define exactly how you will sell your jewelry.

C. Competition - If you have done your homework, you already know that you will have lots of competition with your jewelry. Don't let this discourage you. Instead let it inspire you. Use other designers to motivate and direct your own style. In this section I want you to describe your competitors. Make a file to keep any relevant information about them, including business cards, brochures and Web site URLs. Make sure you include the average price points of each designer in your file. Ask yourself these questions:

- Will your designs be fresher than your competitor's?

- Will you know where your nearest competitors are selling?

- Will you know your competitor's strengths and weaknesses?

- Will you do an assessment of how your competitors business is doing?

- Do you think there is a demand, or that you could create a demand, for your product?

Write up a clear and realistic appraisal to include these points. Include how you plan to outsell your competition or how you plan to compete with them. Unlike other sections in your business plan, this section will require constant work because your competitors will be constantly changing. Utilize catalogs, Internet companies, and your local suppliers in your constant quest to stay price competitive. I think the best way to compete is by creating your own niche with style and creativity.

D. Operating procedure - In this section include how you plan to produce your product for sale. Include how many hours you will work and your projected output. Will you be designing full time or using your spare time after work. Again, I want you to set a realistic goal-something that you know you can live with. If you know you can put in only ten hours a week, set up your plan using eight hours and if you go over, that's good; but at least if you have unforeseen events (as is life) you would already have allotted for that time. Include in your operating procedures whether you will be producing your jewelry alone or with help.

E. Personnel - Most designers start out solo, but at some point you may want to hire an assistant or part time helpers. If you will be designing alone, forget this section of the plan and come back to it when you add employees. If you have employees, you will have to decide how to pay them. You can either pay by the hour or by the piece. Be sure to check your state's wage and employee guidelines. Paying by the piece or piecework may not be legal in your state; nevertheless I used the piece method to set up my hourly wage by timing the amount of time each piece took. I would then use this as a guide to determine how much per hour I paid, holding my employees responsible for working in a timely manner. So even though I wasn't paying by the piece, my hourly wage was governed by how fast the piece could be produced. If you have done a good job of timing yourself with the original samples as we discussed in an earlier chapter, when you give the piece to your helper you will have a fairly accurate accounting of how much time the item takes. Whenever I hired a new employee, I would impress upon them that their work would be judged by how timely and how well each piece was assembled. Our quality control person would check all pieces before they were logged in as finished. When you're ready, open a separate bank account for your business and hire a payroll service. I think you will find this service a necessity, especially since more than likely you will have employee turnover. In my design business I normally employed 10-12 employees, but before and during holiday season, my employees would swell to over 25. Using a payroll service made these adjustments less stressful. By using a payroll service, what could have been a nightmare was a breeze. Letting an expert keep up with deductions for state and federal withholding left me with a clear mind so that I could concentrate on what I did best…designing. At the end of the year my payroll service would also prepare my tax records and keep me on top of the whole nightmare of dealing with federal and state requirements.

F. Summary - Include a mission statement, your business goals & objectives: this section is fairly self-explanatory. Include all your ultimate goals and objectives in brief concise sentences.

Let's move on to the second part of our business plan.

PART II – FINANCIAL DATA BREAKDOWN

A. Finances -This is a big one. How do you plan to finance your business? Will you keep your present job while you get samples together and then sell your designs? Will you get financing from a relative or friend? If you will be securing financing from a friend, relative or investor, this is where you would list your credentials. Include any previous design experience or management skills. In this section, you should also itemize a detailed plan of action explaining how all of the money will be used. Be sure to refer to the next chapter on financing & factoring.

B. Supply list - In this section I want you to list the price and supplier of items that you will need on a regular basis. Include whatever your staple items will be; for instance if you are a metalsmither and you use sterling and gold-filled sheets and wire, this is where you would list your suppliers. This section may change from season to season or within seasons, since more than likely you will find better or cheaper suppliers. Keeping your price points low and profit high should be your primary focus; however don't let price points be the only criteria when dealing with suppliers. I have one supplier I work with on a regular basis whose price points are slightly higher but because of their excellent customer service and exceptional reliability I have given them my business for years.

C. Budget - Be realistic in setting up your budget. I know this will change as you go, but have some idea of how much money you want to spend on certain items within a specified period. I usually set my budget up in three-month intervals. Maybe you'd like to buy your sterling headpins by the pound to get a better price point but if buying them this way will totally throw off your budget you may have to continue buying them in smaller quantities. This section is also where you would include your advertising budget. Even if it's a tiny amount, include it. Do come up with some sort of advertising and promotional plan along with whatever advertising and promotional materials you plan to use. Be sure to include what advertising media you will use and an estimate on the cost of each medium. Your Web site and the costs involved in keeping it up should be in this section along with any tradeshows or craft fair fees and costs associated with them.

D. Balance sheet - Don't let this formal title throw you out of balance. This can be easily and quickly prepared and it really helps you to see just where your business is, in writing. A balance sheet is simply a statement of your financial worth. You can also look at it as a "snapshot" of your business. It should have two parts, assets on the left-hand ("credit") side and liabilities on the right-hand ("debit") side. Assets are things your business owns. This can include money in hand or owed to you, including any account receivables, it can also include any inventory (i.e. necklaces, beads, stones etc., and their worth. Assets can also include things like your studio equipment or jewelers bench.

On the debit side, include your liabilities. Liabilities include any fixed expenses, like your visa merchant account, your rep's showroom fees, rent and payroll, if any. This side will include any long-term debts or monies owed.

The difference between the totals on your balance sheet is your owner's equity or net worth. Assets = liabilities + net worth/owner's equity. An example of a simple balance sheet for Polka Dot jewelry is included in the sample business plan that follows this chapter.

E. <u>Break-even Analysis/Income Projection</u> - I wouldn't worry a lot about this section unless you are securing outside financing. If you are, your investors will want a projection of when and how long you will need to reach a point at which your business will be profitable. You will need to have a fairly accurate estimation of your variable expenses. Once you know what your variable costs are, as well as your fixed cost, you will be able to determine your break-even point. Income Projection - This is called quesstimation...figure out what you think you will make in a year if you follow your business plan in full...Dream Big!!!

F. Summary - This section should be first in your business plan, but you should write it last because, just as the name implies, it summarizes the entire contents of your business plan. I want you to make sure that it is comprehensive and well-written; don't leave out any details. In this section include your goals and objectives. First-time business plan writers often confuse goals and objectives. Remember that goals are things your company wants to achieve while your objectives are how you plan to do it.

I want you to make adjustments to your business plan as you go but don't change it every time you think you've discovered a new supplier or an easier way to do something. Likewise don't change it because you've sold a huge amount of jewelry or sold none at all.

The following business plan for "Pink Polka Dot Jewelry" is an example of how your business plan should look.

SAMPLE BUSINESS PLAN

DESCRIPTION OF BUSINESS

My business name is Pink Polka Dot Jewelry. I plan to market a complete line of infant and toddler accessories. The line will include beaded hair ornaments with future items to include bracelets, earrings and necklaces. I will use good-quality materials, including crystal and vintage or vintage-looking beads to give my line a distinct and unique look with an overall vintage feel. The projected plan is to work at home for the first year and expand my business to a working studio with employees helping with production of the line. I will create all original samples.

MARKETING/SELLING PLAN

My customers will be children's boutiques. I will secure one local rep to sell to this target market. After securing home-based accounts, I will expand my representation to include the southeast section of the United States, and later expand to include eight reps. I will also sell the line on the Internet through our Web site. I will promote the Web site through wholesale tradeshows and retail craft shows.

COMPETITION

I have composed a file of my competitors along with their Web sites and the location of their companies (see attachment). I've taken the time to analyze their strengths and weaknesses. At the current time there is no one in this particular category, especially since our designs will be a combination of fresh, original styling and quality. I plan to out-sell my competitors because of our outstanding designs. Our logo will be composed of baby pink and blue polka dots with our imprinted name inside one of the dots (See our sample logo). I believe that our choice of colors and our eye-catching logo will enhance our line and help us with branding our jewelry. I've lined up a supply of wholesale vendors so our source of supplies can be purchased as close to the source as possible. I've also developed strong business relations with most of the vendors I will be purchasing from. My vendors include _____. I have some professional relationships with reps that have contacts with high-end department stores so that when I feel the line is ready from a production standpoint, I will place the line with them to be sold. I believe that this will also help us solidify and validate our position in the industry, allowing us to outsell our competitors. I've included details of our future Web site structure that will enhance our selling power. My line's visual point-of-sale display will include a logo-enhanced acrylic display and mini pink and blue dot description cards tied to each accessory with pink polka dot ribbon.

OPERATING PROCEDURE/PERSONNEL

For the first 6 months I will be working a total of 20-25 hours a week. My present employment is 20 hours a week. I will keep this position for 6 months in order to put all my earnings into my business. My family has agreed to support me in this endeavor. I will use one employee for approximately 8 hours a week unless demand dictates more. I will operate in the garage of my home, which is currently set up as my design studio. I currently have several weekend shows on my schedule and a rep in mind that understands my financial position and will accommodate me as far as reduced showroom fees and getting new accounts to pay when product is delivered for a percentage reduction off of their total invoice.

SUMMARY

My long-term plan is to be in business for myself. Because of my previous background in working for a top jewelry designer, I believe that I have the business and design skills to be successful. I will use professional representation to sell my line. The reps I am interested in are _____, _____. (List and explain in detail how they will help you.)

I believe that the growth trends in this particular segment of accessories are great, considering the current increase in babies being born to aging baby boomers. Since most boomers have been career oriented and are having babies later in life, they have extra income to spend on their children. I believe that I can create a trend and that the potential of my intended market will be limited only by how much volume I can create.

Because of the unique look of Pink Polka Dot accessories, I believe that I will be able to have a price point on the higher end of the small amount of children's accessories in the market place. To expand from boutiques to higher end department stores is our ultimate long-term goal. Our primary objective is to build a market that is not entirely based on price, but on quality and well thought-out creative designs.

By the end of two years my goal is to have four or more employees. My annual revenue projection is $100,000 or more.

FINANCES

I will use all monies from my part time job to help finance my business. The total amount of money from me that will be put into this venture is $5,000. I will secure matching funds from my parents in the amount of $5,000. I will provide them with a detailed, notarized document of my repayment plan, which will began 15 months from the official start date of my business. The total money in my starting budget will be $10,000.

THE FOLLOWING CHARTS REPRESENT ITEMS FOR "PINK POLKA DOT."

SUPPLY LIST	
Companies	**Supplies**
Acme Supply	Barrette findings
Softflex	Beading wire
Aaron Craft Wire	Craft Wire in different gauges
Pudgy Beads	Vintage Beads
M&R Trim	Ribbons/Trims
The Beadhouse	Czech Beads
Super Direct	Glue
Cream coat	Metal paints
Horizontal Floral	Dried/silk flowers

BUDGET FALL QUARTER (3MONTHS)	
Telephone/ Voicemail $30.00/month (For 3 months)	$90.00
Glue/ one case	$120.00
Craft Wire	$80.00
Web Host - $30.00/month (for 3 months)	$90.00
Printing/Business Cards	$40.00
Ribbons/Trims/Floral	$500.00
Beads	$500.00
Metal/Plastic Paints	$135.00
Craft Wire	$80.00
Helper –4 hours a day@$8.00 hr.	$32.00
Barrette Findings	$200.00

ONE - TIME FEES	
Company Banner	$300.00
Telephone Installation	$120.00
6ft Work Table	$65.00
Extra Lighting	$80.00
Jewelry Display Cases	$150.00
Jewelry Display Forms	$150.00
Web site (URL) registration	$20.00 for 1 year
Show Fee/2 Craft Shows	$200.00

BALANCE SHEET EXAMPLE

CURRENT ASSETS		CURRENT LIABILITIES	
CASH	$10,000	WAGES PAYABLE	$200.00
INVENTORY	$6,000	LOAN PAYMENT TO PARENTS	$5,000
TOTAL CURRENT ASSETS	$16,000	TOTAL LIABILITIES	$5,200.00
OWNERS EQUITY/NET WORTH $10,800			

The right hand side of our balance sheet example lists the liabilities and equity in the following order:

- · Current Liabilities = liabilities due and payable now

- · Non-Current Liabilities = debt which will not become due in the next 12 months.

- · Equity/Net Worth = the difference between total assets and total liabilities.

IF YOU ARE TRYING TO OBTAIN OUTSIDE FINANCING YOU WILL WANT TO INCLUDE EXAMPLES OF THE FOLLOWING:

Work Experience Related to My Intended Business

My work experience has been as follows:
1996 – 1999 Position_____ at _____Co.

Describe your work responsibilities in detail: _____

I have included a list of work references and character references as Exhibit A
I have personal contacts in New York & Los Angeles who are ready to assist in the design, production, and packaging of the accessories line.

Personal Background and Education Credentials

My education includes: graduation from _____ high school (class of ____).

My higher education includes a _____ degree earned in _____ at_____, _____ year.

In _____ school I participated in the following activities (student council, student body officer, sorority/fraternity, clubs, etc.) I have also taken the following classes and seminars: _____, and _____.

My hobbies are: _____

Professional Consultants

I feel it is important that my team of professional advisors be in place before I start in business. Here is a list of these professionals:

Attorney: Verna Hart
Accountant: Terry Taylor
Insurance Agent: James Alexander
Banker: Jesse Bradford
Web Developer: Jacquelyn Matthews

Licenses

My accessory company will require the following licenses. I will need to research the requirements for my own location and circumstances:
1. City Hall: Will include the business license department for resale number
2. My accountant will advise me on federal, state and local reporting and licensing requirements when applicable.

Location Criteria

During my start-up phase of approximately 6-12 months, I plan to operate out of my home studio. Once my business is functioning and I have secured adequate accounts and reps I will move to an industrial/manufacturing area to secure studio space of at least 1000 square feet. I will need my intended studio rental to have a short-term lease with options and to be located convenient to my home. I would like a space that would afford me the possibility of expansion space for future growth.

Financing Strategy

My requirements for start-up capital are as follows:
Attached is a list of expenses that I will need to start or finance Pink Polka Dot Jewelry. This list of items includes buying supplies for my initial line. I already have a computer and enough tools for several employees. I will need some money for initial start-up overhead expenses. The expenses are included in the following cash flow projection.

My sources of cash for starting my business are as follows.

Family (loan from my mother)
Myself
Friends

I am prepared to make presentations to potential lenders.

My presentation kit includes:
1. This business plan
2. Personal financial statement and tax returns.
3. I will have a complete spreadsheet of the amount of funds needed along with a payback program. I will furnish potential lenders a cash-flow projection showing sources of repayments and I will be conservative in my projections.

Web site plans

I will create a Web site with shopping carts to implement sales of our products. I plan to do tradeshows and retail shows to promote our name and Web site. I have already registered the name Pinkpolkadot.com. I plan to hire my sister who is a Web designer to design and maintain my site.

The features of the www.pinkpolkadot.com site will include:

- Easy to use and navigate through
- The site will provide detailed information about all items in our line, including colors, materials used and measurements

E-Commerce Budgeting

The budget for designing and starting our Web site will be nominal _____. This is based on a contract with my sister who is a Web designer. The estimated monthly maintenance cost to support the site will be $ _____.

E-Commerce Competition

I feel the need for a Web site is not only an industry standard but is an absolutely necessary marketing tool. The Pink Polka Dot site will be youthful, fresh and tastefully done.

LOCATION CRITERIA

During my start-up phase of approximately 6-12 months, I plan to operate out of my home studio. Once my business is functioning and I have secured adequate accounts and reps, I will move to an industrial or manu-factoring area to secure studio space of at least 1,000 square feet. I will need my intended studio rental to have a short-term lease with options and to be located convenient to my home. I would like a space that would afford me the possibility of expansion space for future growth.

FINANCING STRATEGY

My requirements for start-up capital are as follows:

Attached is a list of expenses that I will incur to start or finance Pink Polka Dot Jewelry. This list of items includes buying supplies for my initial line. I already have a computer and enough tools for several employees. I will need some money for initial start-up overhead expenses. The expenses are included in the following cash-flow projection.

MY SOURCES OF CASH FOR STARTING MY BUSINESS ARE AS FOLLOWS.

Family (loan from my mother)

Myself

Friends

I AM PREPARED TO MAKE PRESENTATIONS TO POTENTIAL LENDERS.

My presentation kit includes:

1. This business plan
2. Personal financial statement and tax returns.
3. I will have a complete spreadsheet of the amount of funds needed, along with a payment program. I will furnish potential lenders a cash-flow projection showing sources of repayments and I will be conservative in my projections.

WEB SITE PLANS

I will create a Web site with shopping carts to implement sales of our products. I plan to do trade and retail shows to promote our name and Web site. I have already registered the name Pinkpolkadot.com. I plan to hire my sister who is a web designer to design and maintain my site.

THE FEATURES OF THE WWW.PINKPOLKADOT.COM SITE WILL INCLUDE:

· Easy to use and navigate through
· The site will provide detailed information about all items in our line, including colors, materials used and measurements

E-COMMERCE BUDGETING

The budget for designing and starting our Web site will be nominal _____. This is based on a contract with my sister who is a web designer. The estimated monthly maintenance cost to support the site will be $ _____.

E-COMMERCE COMPETITION

I feel the need for a Web site is not only an industry standard but is an absolutely necessary marketing tool. The Pink Polka Dot site will be youthful, fresh and tastefully done.

ဖာကဖာကဖာကဖာကဖာက

Inspirational quote: "We may affirm absolutely that nothing great in the world has been accomplished without passion," HEGEL 1832.

CHAPTER 5

FINANCING & FACTORING

In a previous chapter we briefly mentioned the most obvious ways to get financing for your line, such as family, friends or your savings. If you're fortunate enough to have any of the above you are in a terrific position. Having resources like these can make the finances of your new business less stressful. Most accessory lines are started with very little capital. One question I'm always asked is, "how do you get monies to finance your business?"

When I first started my line, I had almost no working capital. The only way I was able to accumulate funds to buy supplies was to encourage my rep to send as many orders C.O.D. as she could. This way, within seven days I would receive full payment. I would then invest all monies received, in the next orders. To encourage your accounts to pay C.O.D., offer incentives, like discounts on the total order. If it's a boutique you have not previously worked with, offer the first order C.O.D. and all orders after that on a net-30 basis, after you or your rep have checked their references. Be creative, think of ways you can "grow your company" to become financially stable.

The following suggestions can help you finance your business.

1. **Borrow from yourself** – If you have lines of credit on your credit cards you might be able to use advances to help you get your line off the ground. But before you run out and start charging, make sure you've read through the chapter on writing a business plan. Don't start to use your line of credit until you finish your plan and work up a budget. Analyze your plan to make sure you have thoroughly taken into account the best-and worst-case scenario. The best being that, everything goes as planned and you get the amount of sales you want and the worst being that you get no sales. This is where having back-up

plans of marketing in place will help. Because you can pay a monthly minimum amount on your cards, if you are frugal and have truly decided that you are willing to put in the time required to sell your jewelry, this may be a viable option for you. Having a regular form of employment is an asset when financing your business this way. If you have a relationship with a commercial bank you might be able to open a revolving line of credit. This type of credit will give you a fixed amount of credit and as the funds are used, the "credit line" is reduced and when payments are made the line is replenished. One major advantage of this type of credit is that no interest is accrued until the funds are withdrawn.

2. **Borrow from friends and relatives** – Is your first thought on this "they wouldn't loan me money" or "why would anyone loan me money?" trust me, they won't if they feel you are just giving the whole idea of a jewelry business lip service. Have you explained and shared your marketing plan with them? Have you showed them examples of your jewelry? Have you shared examples of someone you know who is successful and making money with their craft? Have you shared your long-term business plan with them? Do they truly know the potential of your proposed business? Have you always been a person who followed through on what you started or do you quit when the going gets tough and your family and friends know this? These are all things you should consider when you ask for assistance in financing your business. You could ask for a loan or form a limited partnership where your investors would earn a percentage of the businesses profits. If you are fortunate enough to use someone else's money, just make sure everything is put in writing, along with a repayment plan. Oops, forgot to mention, make sure you tell them, and put it in writing, that their investment doesn't give them carte blanche to tell you how to run things. Having back-seat

drivers trying to tell you how to run your business is the same as having them tell you how to drive a car.

3. **Suppliers** – I bet you never thought of your suppliers in terms of helping you finance your business, but they can. Early on, handpick one or two suppliers of items that you need and purchase from them consistently. Make sure you select a small-to medium-size company; large suppliers will be harder to establish a credit relationship with. Early on, I placed consistent orders with one major supplier of Swarovski crystal and was given a line of credit. After purchasing and paying my invoices on time I was able to parlay my good credit standing to other suppliers that I used. Having 30-60 days before I had to pay for supplies helped me stay in business. My net-30 invoices would at maximum pay me in 60 days, so having credit allowed me to get my orders delivered and pay for the inventory when I got paid. In my line we were using lots of crystal, sometimes up to thirty thousand dollars worth. Without having this kind of credit I wouldn't have been able to get my orders produced. So don't overlook the power of establishing and nurturing any supplier who will extend you credit. After all, having credit is like having money you didn't have.

4. **Microloans** – Small loans up to $10,000 are available for almost any for-profit start-up, newly established or growing small business. This type of financing is available through the SBA. Under this program, the SBA makes funds available to nonprofit community-based lenders called intermediaries, which in term provide loans to eligible borrowers. To qualify for one of these loans you will have to contact the SBA Web site for a list of intermediaries in your local area (see our resource pages). Each intermediary has it own lending and credit requirements, although they all require some type of collateral and a personal guarantee of the business owner. Before a loan is extended,

the intermediary will require you to complete their program of business-based training. Terms for the loan are generally between 8% and 13% for 6 years. I know of only one jewelry designer that got additional financing for her business this way. She used the funds to do higher end shows to grow her customer base. The process for acquiring these loans can be lengthy, so start the application process before you actually need it.

5. **Letters of Credit** – A letter of credit is not really credit; rather it is a guarantee from a bank that a specific amount of money will be honored by the bank if the borrower fails to pay. This type of credit is usually used when dealing with new vendors who have not extended credit to you. The bank simply offers a letter backing up your credit worthiness as assurance to the vendor that you will pay. Although the bank does not pay out any funds, you will have to go through the same procedure as qualifying for a loan…check with your local bank for details.

6. **Unsecured lines of credit** – There are many companies out there that offer unsecured lines of credit. Each company has different requirements. We have included a few companies on our resource pages to get you started.

7. **Factoring** - I wanted to devote some space to factoring. Factoring is when you get an advance against money owed to you from a boutique or department store. Factors are primarily used after your business is established and when you have purchase orders from well-known department stores or boutiques. It can provide a business with the cash flow needed to continue their business. Most companies use a factorer only when it is absolutely necessary, because of the fees involved. Before your company can obtain the services of a factor you will have to provide a profile of you and your company. A profile usually includes personal information including a credit rating, location of your

business, years in business, amount of invoices per year and clients (boutiques & department stores you work with). The factorer is usually some type of financial institution. Before they will advance you money they usually investigate your potential customer's (boutique or department store) debt-and-payment patterns to their creditors as well as your customer's financial strength before they give you the go-ahead to proceed with the order. Once the factorer decides the credit-worthiness of your customer, you can then manufacture and/or ship your merchandise to the customer (boutiques or dept. store). You will have access to about 70% to 80% of the monies from the original invoice.

The Two types of factoring: "full-factoring" and "non-notification."

❑ In "full-factoring," the factor performs all communications and operations pertaining to money with your customer (boutique or dept. store), from the beginning to the end of the order. For their services, factors usually charge an average of .70% to 1.30% of the gross of each order. If an order was for $100,000 and the factor charged 1.3%, you (the manufacturer), would receive $100,000 minus $1300, for a total of $98,000. At this point the factorer will advance you approximately 70% to 80% of the $98,000. On small orders, the percentage the factorer receives is usually much larger so it may not be cost effective for you to use their services on small orders.

❑ The second type of factoring is called "non-notification." The percentages of monies advanced and the procedure is the same as in full factoring. The one difference is that the manufacturer deals with his customer until the customer becomes seriously delinquent in paying the invoice, in which case the factor steps in and deals with the delinquent customer. The fees for this type of factoring are usually cheaper than "full-factoring."

DUNN & BRADSTREET

Dunn & Bradstreet's relationship to businesses is the same as Equifax's or Experian's relationship to the average consumer's credit report; both organizations keep files and records on their clients such as payment histories and patterns, amount of debt owed and property owned such as land, buildings, and equipment.

You must have to have a Dunn & Bradstreet number before you can work with any major department store. To get an account or identification number you will need to supply them with the name, address, telephone number, number of employees, and any other relevant information needed. They will then issue your company a permanent D&B number that becomes your identification number.

When your design company applies for credit with a supplier, the supplier may contact Dunn & Bradstreet to see what their files contain on your company. If no negative information is found, such as late payments, court judgments, collection-agency activity, etc., your company may receive an open account status (credit to purchase now on the promise to pay later).

You can also contact Dunn & Bradstreet when you need information on a new customer (boutique or store). Before you manufacture or ship a particular order, it is a good idea to get a rating, especially if your rep has no information on the client (store/boutique). Our resource page has Dunn & Bradstreet's contact information.

ॐ·ॐ ॐ·ॐ ॐ·ॐ ॐ·ॐ ॐ·ॐ

Inspirational Quote: "Without a doubt, the worst thing in life is not failing to reach your goals, it's not having goals to reach!"

CHAPTER 6

WHAT YOU WILL NEED BEFORE YOU SELL

A s you can see, the business of starting and managing your business has many layers, including deciding what type of jewelry to make, how to get financing, how and who to hire to help with your bookkeeping and maintaining your Web site-and the list goes on and on. Let's not forget that the fundamental thing you want to do is to sell your jewelry for a profit. Deciding how you want to go about selling your product is primary but before we get into the many ways of selling, there are some important tools you will need-regardless of what method you choose to sell. Accepting charge cards is a tool that will enhance your sales, whether you sell at craft fairs, on your Web site or wholesale to your own boutique accounts. Accepting credit cards is not only a quick and easy way for your customers to pay for their purchases; it also gives advantages to you as a merchant. Potential customers will often spend more freely when they know they can charge their purchases and will spend more on impulse items.

The following chapter will help you navigate through the maze of setting up a merchants account. First, let's define exactly what a merchants account is. A merchant's account is simply an account that allows a merchant (that's you) to accept credit card payments, either in a real-world setting with a card swiper or online. Setting up an account can be confusing when sorting through the seemingly unlimited number of providers. Hopefully this chapter will give you a better understanding of how the process works.

SETTING UP A MERCHANTS ACCOUNT

Types of Processors

There are several types of companies that will set up your merchant account:

Bank - Your current bank is a reliable place in which to set up your account. Most banks offer extra benefits to their business accounts, including Merchant Services. However, most banks do not process credit card transactions themselves; they turn this procedure over to a third party. To get approved at your bank is oftentimes tougher than in other channels. So if you are a new or small business, the application and approval process might be more complicated.

Third Party Credit Card Processors - Third party credit card processors dedicate themselves to handling credit card processing. By using a third party to process your charges they will be responsible for every aspect of the process including authorization, billing, reporting, and settlement.

Independent Sales Organization - An independent sales organization (ISO) is a registered credit card merchant broker. These organizations usually represent several third-party credit card processors. They set up and service credit card merchants, but do not do the actual card processing. Getting approved through an ISO is easier than going through a bank, but you will pay more to set up and process your merchant account. Another important point to remember is that ISOs are not as strictly regulated as banks, so use caution when selecting one.

Trade Associations/Warehouse Retailers - Warehouse retailers and trade associations often offer credit card merchant processing at discount prices. This may be a good resource for jewelry manufacturers, since this business is usually viewed as a cottage industry business.

Tip: MasterCard and Visa require you to establish a merchant account through one of the above; however, with American Express and Discover you can apply directly to them.

BEFORE SETTING UP YOUR ACCOUNT

1. Before any provider sets up a merchant account for you, they will want to make sure that you are a legitimate business. Usually they will start with a credit check of the owner or owners listed on the application. Having two or three credit references from suppliers you use will help with your approval. Providers do credit and background checks to protect them from illegal fraudulent charges.

2. The most important question that provider's want answered is whether your business is likely to have a high incidence of charge backs on your merchant account. Charge backs are when customers dispute or cancel a charge. This can happen if the customer is unhappy with the purchase or they were charged the wrong amount. Charge backs can create charge back fees and a loss of the funds.

3. Another important aspect to securing a merchant account is the type of credit card transactions that your company will be processing. Tangible goods, like jewelry are much safer and less risky than service businesses. Also, credit card transactions where you obtain a signature are considered safer than phone, Internet, or mail orders. You will still be able to get a merchant account if you do business any of these ways but your processing costs will be higher.

WHAT YOU NEED TO GET STARTED - A TERMINAL

For card-present transactions, the biggest up-front cost will be for the machine used to swipe cards, which is called a terminal. Basic terminals cost between $200 and $1,200. Options include the traditional point-of-sale retail credit card machines and wireless credit card processors that work like cell phones for those who sell at shows. There are also many software solutions for those who sell and process their credit cards on the Internet. If you get a terminal with a printer or a wireless terminal you will have to pay more. You may want to lease a terminal instead. Keep in mind that the price of leases varies widely, so make sure you pay attention to the small print.

Terminals are not required for card-absent transactions; instead, you can get software that will verify transactions from your PC or laptop at very reasonable prices. Some providers even support card verification directly over the phone.

WHERE YOU WILL SPEND YOUR MONEY:

You will have to pay an application fee. Some credit card payment system providers charge application fees of up to $200 and they can be non-refundable, even if they turn you down for an account. You may also have to pay setup or account-activation fees. Make sure you understand exactly what you will be paying for before you sign anything. Some providers may say they do not have certain fees, but watch out for the higher percentages in other parts of their services.

The primary fee on credit card payment-systems is the discount rate or transaction fee. This fee is the percentage the credit card payment-systems providers charge on each transaction you do. Banks and larger credit card payment-system providers will base this fee on information you provided in your application like:

. Your average ticket sales

. The type of transaction you will be processing (card present or absent).

. Charge-volume, the yearly amount you plan on processing.

Because of the difference in risk, most providers will have two different rates. One rate will be when the credit card is present. Another rate will be for mail/telephone orders-this includes Internet transactions. This rate

66

will be applied any time the card is absent from the transaction. Card-present transaction discount rates can range from 1.5% to 2%. Card-absent transactions can range from 2.2% to 3.0%.

Another processing fee charged by the merchant bank is the "per transaction" fee. This fee is generally $0.20 to $0.30 for card-present transactions and $0.30 to $0.50 for card-absent transactions. There is also a fee to cover the cost of issuing monthly credit card transaction summaries, usually around $10.

Some provider's tact on additional fees to the basic fees, including annual fees, programming fees, shipping/handling fees, Internet processing fees, customer support fees, and set-up fees. Remember that these are merely ways for them to make extra money. These processors really want more money, but in order to seem more competitive they may keep the up-front fees on par with their competitor's but they tack on other fees.

Questions you should ask each provider

1. Is there a set-up or application fee? If there is, you may want to shop around for someone who doesn't charge this fee.

2. Is there a monthly or annual fee? Again, shop around. Some companies don't charge these fees.

3. What percentage does the provider take from your sale with card-present and card-absent transactions? For large credit card volume amounts you might try to negotiate a reduced per-transaction rate.

4. What is the charge-back fee? Again, this is what they charge if your customer decides not to accept a transaction. Make sure you get an outline of your rights and how to respond to claims against you.

5. Do they offer 24/7 live customer service support? I prefer live support. If they don't have it, find out how quick the turnaround reply is for e-

mail questions. Good customer service is very important and the lack of it can negatively impact you. Ask for customer referrals from their current clients with businesses that are equal to yours in volume. When you contact these clients ask them how long they usually have to wait for a customer service rep? Are their problems dealt with quickly and professionally? How do they deal with charge-backs and are there any charges for support calls?

6. Which credit cards (Visa, MasterCard, Diners, etc.) do they process? The more cards you can accept, the more sales you are likely to have.

7. You will be asked to estimate your monthly sales, please be conservative. If you estimate a high volume of transactions, you may be asked to keep a percentage (up to a full month) of estimated order totals in an account to cover possible fraud.

8. Since providers differ on how long it may take for funds to be deposited into your account, be sure to ask how long it takes for funds to be transferred. Be sure to tell them if your transactions will be retail/credit-card present or Internet/mail-order/telephone, credit-card absent. Mail-order/Internet transactions usually take longer to process.

IMPORTANT TIPS

- You should display your company's policy at the point of purchase explaining to customers how they can return merchandise or request credits. You may want to print the policy on your receipts. This will strengthen your case if charges are reversed.

- Compare equipment costs to leases. Prices can vary widely, so make sure you get accurate terminal/model numbers.

- Some providers tout high acceptance rates (99%), but remember, these rates are common among Independent Sales Organizations or ISOs, so don't be fooled.

- If you don't expect to charge more than a couple of thousand dollars a month, try to negotiate a lower monthly and set-up fee.

- Watch out for long-term leases with early termination fees, you should be able to switch providers if you want.

- Keep your eyes open for those low introductory rates that increase after a few months.

- If you are not using a major bank/warehouse club or financial institution you recognize, make sure you check out the company you're considering, to make sure they are legitimate. There are fake processing companies that collect set-up fees and vanish. I would definitely contact the Better Business Bureau to check out the company's status. If you find your provider on the web, ease your mind by getting a physical address and telephone number.

- Get the whole picture. Know all the fees your provider will charge. In short, get the complete picture of the total costs before making your final decision. And remember, "Get it in writing."

- To help you in your search for a provider, search around, ask people you know or vendors you see at craft shows who they use and what problems they have had, if any?

- **READ YOUR CONTRACT...READ YOUR CONTRACT**. Make sure you understand all the small print. This includes your minimum charges, fees, terms of your agreement and termination clauses. Be sure to go over this with your provider to make sure you have the facts.

SETTING UP A MERCHANT ACCOUNT FOR INTERNET ORDERS

If you will be using your Merchants Account for web orders, I've included some tips and information that may help you get started.

1. One of the main disadvantages you will have when doing business online is that you won't have the option of examining the signature or requesting additional identification. If you think an order you've received online may be fraudulent, you should ask the customer to confirm the transaction by requiring them to send proof by mail or fax that they made the purchase. If you sense some hesitation on their part, point out that the additional proof of purchase is for their protection. This is one way of avoiding the "charge-back" factor. This simply means that if the credit card you accepted was fraudulent you will lose the money for the sale and will have to pay the bank a charge-back fee (these fees can vary from $10 - $25). Fraudulent credit-card use is more prevalent on the Internet than it is when the card is present. When accepting credit cards by mail order of any type, you can't match up the signature on the back of the card to the customer's current signature and you can't ask for a form of picture identification. An online merchant can cut down the risks of credit-card fraud by getting the CVV2 number. The CVV2 number is the three or four digit number on the back of the card.

2. You might want to include your Web site address on your card printout, along with your company name. This will help your customer eliminate any possible confusion with their credit-card transaction statement.

3. If you process cards on your site, make sure you have a secure server. A secure server is one that can encrypt credit-card information. You should find a credit-card provider that offers secure ordering through SSL (secure socket layer), a widely used web security standard.

MERCHANT ACCOUNTS WITHOUT TERMINAL RENTALS

It is possible to accept credit cards over the Internet and in person without establishing your own merchant account. These third-party merchants have no setup fees, no monthly fees and give you free web payment tools. They typically batch your money into regularly scheduled payments, which can be inconvenient because they deposit your money into your account slower. In addition, their rates tend to be significantly higher. However, you can set up these accounts without credit checks or long drawn-out applications. The leading third-party merchants are Paypal, Propay, and CCBill.

MAJOR THIRD-PARTY TERMINAL-FREE PROCESSORS.

PAYPAL

PayPal is an all-in-one payment solution. PayPal allows you to accept credit cards, debit cards, bank transfers and PayPal account balances. With Paypal you can receive real-time notification. Real-time notification simply means that as soon as a payment is made it will be reflected in your account. With Paypal you can process payments online (accept all major credit cards, debit cards, instant bank transfers and PayPal through your Web site or e-mail). Paypal's Payment Pro has a virtual terminal that allows you to do online what you would do if you had a credit card processing machine. So you are instantly saving money by not having to invest in a terminal. The setup for your Web site is quick and easy, with no downtime required for your site. The negative is that the transaction fees are slightly higher than setting up your own individual account, but you have none of the other expenses.

PROPAY

Whereas Paypal is used mostly for Internet and Web site processing, Propay is used primarily for accepting credit card payments in person. They usually process your payments fast and provide excellent customer support. There are no application fees, monthly fees, minimum fees or cancellation fees. They do have a small annual fee. Their per-transaction fee is very reasonable and of course there are no equipment purchases. At a craft fair or venue, you would simply enter your customer's credit card information using a laptop through Propay's Web site or with a touchtone or cell-phone.

To process a customer's credit card, you will need to collect:

- ✓ Credit Card Number
- ✓ Card Expiration Date
- ✓ Zip Code
- ✓ Transaction Amount

Once you enter this information, ProPay will give you an immediate authorization or decline. Funds are usually deposited into your account within 1-3 business days (depending on your account type). You can go online and log into your account to see your available funds and your balance at anytime. With Propay you can transfer your funds to your checking account or to a MasterCard debit card that Propay offers.

ProPay is the easiest available way to process credit cards. With no sign up, monthly, or equipment fees, this is definitely a low-risk, low-cost way to start accepting credit cards. I have a friend who uses her laptop at craft fairs. She uses an air card to connect with the Internet.

Previously we mentioned that some traditional merchant processors may try to lure you with low rates that you probably won't qualify for. With ProPay you know what you're paying up-front. If you know anyone who uses this method of accepting credit cards, ask them how happy they are with ProPay's processing rate (how quickly the money in deposited in your account), its fees and its overall customer service.

CCBILL

CCBILL offers an easy, secure way to process credit card transactions, primarily through your Web site. By using CCBill's services, you avoid the up-front expense and time required to set up e-commerce software or a merchant account. CCBill offers great fraud-protection, which keeps transaction charge-backs at a minimum. They provide 24/7 customer-service support. This provider may be what you need if you need just Web site processing and don't plan on doing any in-person processing. They also give you the ability to accept multiple cards including Visa, MasterCard, Discover and Amex.

Tip: We've included some e-commerce sites on our resource pages to help you with your research. Be sure to take your time and note the details of each source.

ഇൗഇൗഇൗഇൗഇൗഇൗ

Inspirational quote: "Dreams without appropriate action remain a dream."

SELLING YOUR WAY TO SUCCESS: THE MANY WAYS OF SELLING!

Now that we've gotten the "how to get your money once it's sold" part of the book out of the way, lets get into the many ways of selling. This is the part of the book where I get excited; growing your business can be exciting. Choosing what way or combination of ways you want to sell is all about you. Maybe you don't have weekends free so doing craft shows is out of the question; you can do home and corporate parties. Maybe you hate marketing; you can find a rep to sell for you, or have your items displayed in a craft mall or online. There are many ways to fit your dream into your current lifestyle. Just keep in mind that the most important part of making your dream a reality is to make a realistic plan and be dogmatic about sticking to it.

CHAPTER 7

SELLING WITH A REP

HOW TO FIND REPRESENTATION (REPS) FOR YOUR LINE

So you're ready for the big time! You've worked out all the bugs in your line; you have a production staff ready and waiting, and you're ready for a representative or "rep." A jewelry rep is an independent sales person who wholesales several lines of jewelry to retail stores and boutiques. They are self-employed and usually represent competing jewelry lines. With a sales rep you will have no control over how or if they sell your line, however they are paid on commission so if they don't show it they won't sell it and they won't make money. Having a rep will allow you to reach geographic markets you couldn't possibly reach on your own. You may choose to have several reps representing you, each with an exclusive area or territory.

If you're in a major metropolitan city, you probably have a fashion mart nearby. Visit the mart in your area, find the accessory floor and do your homework. Every mart has "Market Week" in which you can freely walk in and out of the showrooms. Take advantage of this time to check and compare styles and price points in each showroom. If it is not market week, you won't be able to move around freely, because showroom owners will want your qualifications to gain entry into their showroom. More than likely you will be asked for I.D., including the name and address of your retail store. So if possible visit during market week. You can find out the dates by calling the mart's business office (See our resource page for a list of marts).

Some showrooms are high-end, meaning they carry more expensive accessory lines; therefore price points and client retail stores buying in these showrooms are more upscale. You will also find showrooms that are middle and low end. Sometimes it's hard to determine where a particular showroom fits. The wholesale prices are usually not visible, so you will have to ask. In some showrooms it's easy to figure out who their clientele is, particularly if it's a showroom geared for junior's or tween's. You can usually tell a high-end showroom by the way the merchandise is displayed and by the showroom décor. Evaluate what showroom you think your accessories might fit in with and make a note of that showroom. Never try to talk to showroom managers about representing your line during market week. They will be too busy taking orders and will not have time to talk about acquiring a new line.

During market week, there's usually an area devoted to reps that don't have permanent showrooms. These reps are called "road reps." They usually set up in temporary showrooms. These temporary showrooms can be located in the basement area of the main mart or on an unused floor. If you'd like to locate the area, just ask someone in the reception area of the main entrance to the mart. Employing the services of temporary reps may work out better for you since they travel in a given territory selling to boutiques and stores. In my opinion, road reps generally get more orders for the lines they represent than those who sit in their showrooms waiting for stores to visit them. There are some reps that offer both services, a permanent showroom and road representation. If you can find representation that offers both, you will have the advantage of increased sales. By visiting boutiques and specialty shops, road reps offer more personalized service. From the designer's standpoint, your orders are more consistent and spread out, instead of having all your orders and delivery dates only during market week. Storeowners usually love road reps because they can coordinate accessories with clothing on display, making it much easier to match colors and styles.

Once you've decided which rep you want to contact, wait about two weeks after market week before trying to make an appointment. The first week or so the reps have appointments with stores (buyers) who did not come during the previous week. When calling, be persistent. Remember they are called constantly by new artists seeking representation, but because they make their living selling accessories, acquiring a wonderful new line keeps them profitable....so persistence will payoff.

When you finally have your potential rep on the phone, the first question they usually ask is, "What kind of line do you have?" Be prepared with a good description. Is your line more Victorian than contemporary, more avant-garde than classic? You can bet you'll be asked what price point your line is (see the section on price points), so be prepared with a range of where your line's prices are. Sometimes you will be asked to mail samples along with price points. If you decide to do this, make sure you document what you are sending. You can find information about this in our chapter on consignment. Before you agree to send actual samples, ask if line sheets will do. Line sheets are color copy sheets of your jewelry and wholesale price points.

If you're not in a major city and cannot visit showrooms, call the fashion mart office in the largest city nearest you and ask for a copy of the directory from the previous mart season. The directory will usually list the accessory lines carried and will specify which showroom or rep represents them. Some showrooms or reps may even have page ads with descriptions of the lines they carry, and many will have Web site addresses. This can give you a better idea of how or if your line will fit in. After you've decided which reps to call, ask them if they are interested in acquiring a new line and if it would be possible to send them line sheets of your designs. After you've sent them the sheets, if they haven't contacted you in two weeks, call them. Ask them what they thought about your line and what they liked or disliked about it. If you find out "they love your line" and would like to represent you, congratulations. If you find out they did not like the line, try to find our why. Was it not what their showroom needed because they already had a similar line? Was it your price points? Some reps like to play God and will criticize and verbally tear apart your line. If this happens to you, don't take everything said so seriously and please don't let one or two negative comments discourage you. If on the other hand, the rep offers constructive criticism, listen and thank them for their opinion. Only after careful consideration should you change the design of your line because of a showroom rep's opinion. Trust that whether or not your line is accepted does not reflect on how good or bad it is but rather that the showroom may have a similar line or it just may not fit in that particular showroom. That's why getting detailed explanations of why your line is not accepted is so important. Don't let one or two reps make you give up. If the rep viewing your line is intimidating don't let them intimidate you, just politely thank them for viewing your line sheets. If you mailed actual samples, kindly remind them to mail your samples back in the pre-addressed and stamped packaging you enclosed when you mailed them. At this point you might also ask if they could recommend a showroom (or rep) that might be suitable or interested in your line. Most reps tend to keep in close contact with other showrooms, so they may know just the right place for your accessories.

Be aware that even when sending your line to a "reputable" rep, the business still is very competitive. I had the experience of sending my line to one of the "top" reps in the fashion mart in Los Angeles, only to discover a few months later that all the styles that I sent were copied and reproduced by another manufacturer that the rep already represented. That manufacturer, by the way, was owned by the rep.

Try to discover if a potential rep, represents any lines that they own. In my opinion this is totally unethical and does not promote good will on their part. If this is the case and the time comes to sell or promote a line, whose line do you think will get the most representation? These reps will take your showroom fee for their profit, not caring if you get any orders. This is one of the unfair practices that I've seen. We are not suggesting that all reps do this, just be aware of the possibility.

78

BE PREPARED:

1. SOME SHOWROOMS WILL ASK FOR A SHOWROOM FEE - Usually between $50 and $200 a month. A few years ago this was not as common as it is today, however it is the rule rather than the exception. If you pay a showroom fee you might want to find out just where your jewelry will be displayed in the showroom – sometimes reps take lines for showroom fees with no intention of trying to sell them. Make sure they don't stick your line in the back of the showroom completely hidden from sight of any potential buyer.

2. BE PREPARED TO PAY 15% TO 20% COMMISSION - The average fee is 15%. See our sample forms at the end of the book. With major department stores, an order is not a valid order until you get a P.O. number (purchase order number). Once you have that number, it's your guarantee that you will be paid. Be sure to double check the delivery dates so that your orders are delivered by the deadline.

3. COMMISSION FEES – These fees are usually paid to the rep after you have received payment from the vendor (boutique or dept. store). The fees are usually due the first of the month, for the previous month's billings.

4. IF THE 'REP" WANTS TO REPRESENT YOUR LINE - A contract is usually drawn up. Sign up with a rep that truly wants your line and is excited about it. If a rep is enthusiastic about the line you can bet you will probably get a fair amount of orders.

5. MOST OF THE CONTRACTS ARE RELATIVELY SIMPLE - The rep agrees to sell your line at whatever commission fees you both have decided upon. The contract should also have showroom fees and any other fees clearly spelled out. Don't sign any papers for representation without taking them home to read carefully. Pay attention to the small print. If you have any questions or find something troubling, by all means get a professional to look at your contract. We've included a sample rep contract in our sample forms section.

CONGRATULATIONS, YOU'VE FOUND THE IDEAL REP!

So, you've found the rep you want to represent your line and the rep feels he or she can do a good job for you. Here are some questions and concerns that should be answered before the final contract is drawn:

A. How long has the rep (showroom) been in business?

B. What kind of reputation do they have?

Ask around and try to find other designers, who are familiar with them. To find more detailed information, find the rep in the market week directory. I'm assuming you picked up one when you visited the mart. Check the listing for other designers represented by them. Usually the names of other lines are listed alphabetically. Do some detective work, starting online by typing the name of the line in the browser. Do this for all the lines they represent. You should be able to at least acquire a couple of telephone numbers or e-mail addresses. It's a long shot, but you may have luck on your side. If you do locate some designers, contact them and tell them who you are and that you are thinking about letting their rep carry your accessory line. Assure them your line is totally different from theirs. Ask them how long they've been with the showroom and is there anything you should be prepared to deal with if you sign with them?

✓ **MAKING THE CONNECTION:** From the main mart office, try to secure a back issue of a market week directory from the previous year. Look up your future rep, note if any contact information is available on the designers they no longer represent. If there is no contact information, but the designers' names are listed, try typing their name into your browser to see if they have a Web site. If they have a Web site, you're in luck because every site has a link for contacting them. Ask them why they are no longer with your potential rep. Sometimes

80

you can luck out and get a designer who doesn't mind sharing some relevant information. Use whatever information you get to help you make a final decision.

✓ **BE AWARE OF ANY HIDDEN COSTS:** Ask your potential rep how many and what shows they do a year, and what amount of monies is needed on average for them. Ask what advertising they do and what share you will have to pay and for what size of space. Also ask if the final decision as to whether or not you do the shows or ads is left up to you or is it mandatory? I've had reps hike fees to the designers for shows and ads. For example one rep we had would charge each line $250. At the time they were reping about 20 lines. The total amount of money taken in by the rep was $5,000. The expenses with show fees, transportation, hotel and food might total $2,000, if they were not staying in a "five-star" hotel. These reps immediately made a $3,000 profit at the expense of their designers. I don't have a problem with anyone staying in a five-star hotel, just not with my hard-earned money. In my opinion, this is totally unfair. Not all reps do this, but some do. So, if possible, have an option clause regarding shows and advertising written into your contract.

✓ **HANDING OVER YOUR SAMPLES:** Before you release your samples, make sure they are well-documented. Give each piece a style number and price. Make two inventory sheets, one for the rep, and one for you. Have your rep sign your copy, stating that they received the samples. Have the wholesale value totaled at the bottom of the inventory sheet. Follow this procedure each time you give or take samples to and/or from your rep. By not doing this each time, you may lose inventory, because it's impossible to keep up with how many samples a rep has without it. You may also need this in writing, in case there is ever a discrepancy over how many samples were left in your rep's care (see our consignment chapter).

✓ **AT LEAST 5 TIMES A YEAR, SOMETIMES 7**: You will be asked for new samples for spring, summer, cruise, fall and holiday seasons. In addition to ongoing samples, you may also have multiple demands on an ongoing basis from your rep for special accessory items that they "needed yesterday." Total itemization and signing of new inventory sheets is necessary for these, also. A computer is an asset for this process, because you will be continually modifying and updating your list. Use an Excel spreadsheet to delete or add to your list without having to impute the total document in its entirety. A basic no frills computer can perform these functions perfectly. You or someone on your staff will have to take some time out to learn how to use Excel efficiently. If you already use Excel, you're ahead of the game. If not, learn to use it. In the long run, the money and time saved from mastering this program will be worth every minute.

DEALING WITH THE REP MENTALITY

Reps play an important role in getting your accessories to the right department store or boutique. But an accessory rep without a good designer is not in business. Even reps that pride themselves in being good in sales have to have a good product. A rep can't get a store or boutique to buy something that the store doesn't think it can sell. If you succeed in getting orders, your designs are a key element in this process. Of course, a rep that is friendly, personable and has good sales techniques can only help a good line sell.

Be aware that some reps can make excessive and oftentimes unnecessary demands on their designers. I've had reps that would demand that I make certain styles and combinations that, in their opinion, will "sell like hotcakes" and they needed the samples yesterday. So I in turn, would drop all work in progress, scramble to do what the rep wanted, ship the items to him/her and wait for the orders to pour in. Two weeks later, after having not received a single order, I would call to find out how many orders had been taken. At that point, I would hear every excuse in the book such as, it was a bad market or we will be getting some orders later. Simply put, reps don't have crystal balls and they can't predict what stores will like.

When you get requests from your reps, use common sense before deciding if you should perform the request. There were times when I would get a request for some combination of colors and shapes that just didn't look or feel right, so instead of trusting my instincts I would carry out the design. When they were finally in the rep's hands, the rep would say it should have been longer, shorter, a different color combination, or any number of things. The moral of this story is, never try to design from another person's design head; it's impossible to execute. If they see something a certain way, they should design it, not you. Doing this usually won't pay off for you and will end up being a waste of your time and money. Remember, designing jewelry is an art form, even if it's a production-line piece. The creative process must be allowed to develop from the designer's mind. Don't ever feel you must grant a special request that you don't think is in your best interest. After all, a rep-designer relationship is an equal partnership.

TERMINATING AN AGREEMENT

Earlier I stressed the importance of getting signed copies each time you give samples to your rep. In the beginning of my designing career, I didn't get proper documentation. I didn't keep up with the proper paperwork each time samples were exchanged, or deleted. This was the procedure most designers followed. The reason most of us design is for creative and financial gains, not to become attorneys.

When I decided to terminate my Los Angeles rep-designer agreement, I expressed a verbal and written demand to end our relationship after three years. According to the contract, I had 30 days to settle all monies in order to receive my samples. At the end of the 30 days because of a barrage of orders from other reps, the deadline went unnoticed. When I realized the date had passed, it was about a week past the 30-day deadline. I had also failed to refresh myself with the fine print on the contract. When talking with the rep about outstanding commissions and picking up my samples, I was abruptly informed that all of my samples had been sold for $210. The samples were valued at more than $3,800. My rep then informed me that the commission monies I owed ($2000) were now due. We ended up in court and the rep won the case, with me having to pay the $2,000, and, of course, I had no samples.

There were two reasons why the rep won. One was because I had not received a signed sample sheet each time samples changed hands; therefore I couldn't prove to the judge how many samples were actually in the reps possession, nor the value of them. Two, in the original contract (in small print) was a stipulation clause that stated that upon termination, if debts had not been settled within 30 days, the rep had the right to sell the samples at what ever cost was they decided on. In a court of law all that matters is what's in writing, nothing else. Looking back at this clause now, it is impossible to settle on all monies in 30 days because a designer can receive payments from stores for up to six months. You don't want to pay a rep a commission on a payment you haven't or may not receive. I had this bad experience only once. My other experiences with more than 20 reps nationwide were positive and problem-free. When it was time we were able to terminate our relationship on amicable terms.

ORDERS

After your rep has taken your orders, he/she will usually e-mail, mail or fax them to you. E-mail and faxing will enable you and your rep to speed up the process of you getting your orders in hand. After you receive them you may need to speak directly with the rep to clarify anything that is not clear to you. Try to push for a four-to six-week delivery date, especially on large orders. This will allow you plenty of time for ordering parts not in stock and for production of the pieces. One thing that can't be stressed enough is the importance of delivery dates. All of the work and expense in preparing an order can be a total loss if the order is not in the designated warehouse or receiver station by the due date. This is especially true when working with major department stores. It is much better to ship in advance so your orders arrive a little early, but no earlier than two days before the specified date.

Sometimes reps will push for delivery dates sooner than four to six weeks because they are focused on the bottom line...their commission. The sooner the delivery date, the sooner they will get paid. It's wonderful to accommodate the rep and store if you can, but don't overestimate your abilities. Allow plenty of time to do your best work and to work through any unplanned disasters. I've had reps write an order with a four-week delivery time and I would actually receive the order one and a half to two weeks after the order was written. This would leave me with only two weeks to produce and deliver the merchandise. You've got to make your reps understand the importance of getting your orders to you as soon as possible.

Boutiques are usually more flexible and forgiving of missed deadlines. This does not mean that you can take your time, ignoring the deadlines. Remember, whenever you are late, you have given your customer (boutique), a viable reason to refuse your order.

SHIPPING AN ORDER

You can ship your accessories by U.P.S. (United Parcel Service), Federal Express, Fed-Ex ground, U.S. Mail or any other major courier you may choose. We recommend Fed-Ex ground because they seem to provide the most economical shipping fees. Once your business is shipping over two or three packages a week, you might want to consider getting an account with them. They will pick up your packages daily for shipping, relieving you of having to hand-deliver them to the shipping office. The fee for this convenience is relatively inexpensive and you will be billed on a monthly basis.

Proof of delivery is very important when shipping to any store, large or small. Fed-Ex and U.P.S. does require this and both offer automatic insurance with a value of $100 or less. An additional small fee is charged for each additional $100 value placed on the package. This is excellent coverage, in case your box is lost or destroyed, or for whatever reason it never arrives at the intended destination.

Please compare rates of all the carriers, for the best value.

C.O.D. OR NET 30

YOUR ORDERS WILL BE SOLD BY COD OR NET 30:

Cash On Delivery - For C.O.D. orders, you will most likely be shipping through UPS or Fed-EX. The carrier will be paid upon the orders arrival. The store receiving the order will be required to pay by check. The check is usually forwarded to you within seven business days. In the beginning of my designing career, almost all of my orders were C.O.D.; C.O.D. is a great way to generate money for a poorly financed business. Today, not as many stores will pay on a C.O.D. basis, but it's still okay to ask. Offer some sort of monetary incentive (discount) if they choose to pay this way.

NET-30 - Your customer has 30 days to pay, after having received your merchandise. However, most customers end up paying closer to 60 days. As a manufacturer, remember that whenever you extend these types of terms you will need to pay special attention to your finances, balancing your monies, to make sure you always have enough to cover your ongoing operating expenses. Whenever a possible client (store/boutique) requests net-30 terms, make sure you or your rep have asked for references and checked them. You might also check with Dunn and Bradstreet for their credit rating. (see the section on Dunn and Bradstreet and their contact information on our resource page).

RETURNS AND CREDITS

With boutiques and specialty stores you will be expected to repair items that are returned. However, all major department stores operate on a credit or charge back system. This system allows the store to send whatever accessories it chooses back to you. This is supposed to include accessories that are in need of repair only. You (the vendor) are then required to give a full credit (the wholesale price) back to the store (in short, buy your accessory back from the store you sold it to). Now this would not be all bad if some stores didn't play tricks or allow customers to return items for any reason at all.

There are some customers who make a profession out of choosing expensive items in high end stores, wearing and then returning the items back to the store for a full credit. We call them professional "BWRs" they buy it, wear it and return it. It's like they have an entire department store for rentals without rental fees. If they put the item on their charge card they make sure they return it before the billing date, that way they are not even charged interest on the amount of the charge.

Some professional "BWR's" get entire outfits, head-to-toe, with no intention of keeping them. Maybe if these people knew that it was the small designer who ended up absorbing their flamboyance and not the stores, they would think twice before indulging in this practice.

I recently heard from a rather reliable source that some of the majors were starting to become aware of the professional "BWR's". They have started connecting earrings and tagging other accessories, so that if they are tampered with, disconnected, or the tags are removed, the items could not be returned for a full credit. I believe the day will come when all department stores and boutiques will follow suit and realize that no one wins when people are allowed to abuse the system in this way.

Another unpleasant experience I had involving credits and returns involved a large order from a major department store. The order was shipped to over 75 stores. Several different styles were included in each order. A few weeks after the orders were in the stores we started to receive returns one by one, of the same style. Over a couple of weeks almost all of the 75 stores had returned the same earring, broken in exactly the same place. Needless to say, I was more than a little perplexed. I had an excellent record for quality and had almost no returns on any other orders.

After discussing what was happening with another designer, she informed me that she had the same thing happen to her with the same department store. She then informed me that whenever this particular store chain overbought, or wanted to see what items would sell before paying, they would regularly perform this routine. I'm not saying that this is a common practice, but it did happen to my company and to several other designers I know.

When the major stores return your broken accessories to you, they include an authorization number, which is your way of keeping up with all returns (charge-backs). Be sure to keep a file with all your charge back authorizations in it so that when the charge back is deducted from your accounts payable (monies owed you) by the department store, you will be able to check your records and keep an accurate tally.

ౖ౨ఞ౸ౖ౨ఞ౸ౖ౨ఞ౸ౖ౨ఞ౸ౖ౨ఞ౸

Inspirational Quote: "Our greatest glory is not in never failing, but in rising up every time we fail," Ralph Waldo Emerson.

CHAPTER 8

SELLING YOUR OWN JEWELRY

Selling your own jewelry requires persistence, organizational skills and tough skin. Weather it's you or your rep wholesaling to specialty boutiques and galleries, remember your success depends on selling your jewelry high enough for you to make a good profit and low enough for the store/gallery to make a profit.

As mentioned in an earlier chapter, the usual retail mark-up for stores is at least double, or keystone. Galleries take a commission of anywhere from 15% to 50% and may require you to share in paying rent and utilities. I think the most important question you can ask yourself is, "How much less am I willing to accept for my work so that the shop owner can mark it up and still find buyers?" Keep in mind that a primary advantage of store accounts is that you will be gaining consistent and predictable exposure for your jewelry. Another major advantage of wholesaling is that it will allow you to build up store and clientele loyalty, so that when your items sell you can reap the rewards of repeat orders without expending energy at shows or other venues.

Whatever way you decide to sell, remember to keep what your customers want foremost in your mind. By paying attention, listening and asking questions you will reap the rewards of selling your jewelry and building your business.

IMPORTANT TIPS FOR SELLING YOUR JEWELRY:

❑ Keep abreast of current styles by visiting surrounding shops/boutiques. Keep notes about what, where and how much items similar to yours are selling for in short, learn how to snoop.

❑ Keep in mind just how important having a good name for your company is. Having great names for your products can also help.

❑ Remember your packaging. Making a big deal of this can definitely help your sales. Presentation is almost everything.

❑ Whatever method you choose to sell your jewelry, a great marketing tool is gift certificates. If you sell at home parties or craft fairs, be sure to have your sign prominently displayed. There are many advantages to having gift certificates available, the most obvious is that the recipient has an opportunity to choose exactly what they want and you get a chance to grow your mailing list. Gift certificates will require some record keeping, such as keeping detailed records of each certificate sold. Keeping good records will help you avoid taking in counterfeit or altered ones. Numbering your certificates sequentially will help them easily be accounted for. Print them on unusual paper and imprint them with a unique rubber stamp. Use embossing ink on the customer's copy so that it has raised lettering or a unique raised stamp. Print your duplicate certificates on plain paper. Use clear vinyl sheet protectors to store your original, duplicate and envelops in and file them in a three-ring binder. When someone purchases a certificate, fill in the duplicate copy and keep it for your records. Your gift certificates should provide a space for the purchaser's name, the recipient's name, the date sold, the dollar amount and the date redeemed.

❑ Let potential customers know why your items are special by writing up individual tags with details on what materials you've used in your creations…i.e., beads/glass/vintage/stone, crystals, sterling silver, etc. If you educate people on exactly what they are paying for, you will find less resistance to your prices.

Most importantly, remember that the customers you want are the ones who appreciate what you are selling and are willing to pay your prices. Now lets explore how many other ways there are to sell your product.

SELL TO FRIENDS:

The first and most obvious way to sell, is to sell to friends, especially if you have a large circle of them. Be aware that sometimes selling to people you know can be a trying experience. There is a possibility that your friendship could be put in jeopardy. Oftentimes friends will want special payment plans, freebies, reduced prices, lifetime repairs or special custom orders without a deposit. Because your friends view you as just a friend, making the transition from friend to professional designer may take some getting use to on their part. So practice caution!

SELL TO CO-WORKERS:

Working in a large work environment can be a great outlet to sell your accessories. Wearing your own jewelry and coordinating them with your wardrobe, is the best selling tool you have. It's a surefire way to sell your items without trying. If co-workers want to see your designs and styles, make appointments after work or on your lunch hour. Places of employment usually have strict regulations on promoting or selling items in the workplace so find out what your company guidelines are.

HOME-BASED PARTIES - A GREAT WAY TO SELL

Designers who sell at home-based parties base their parties on the Tupperware principle. Usually they will give the first party themselves, inviting friends and co-workers. Hopefully people attending the party will want to give their own party and sell your jewelry to their friends and relatives. A discount is usually given to the host or hostess (the person giving the party). The designer or the host/hostess will usually provide the party with refreshments.

You and your hostess/host should wear pieces of your jewelry during the party. It's also a good idea to change pieces every 30 minutes or so. Have a good selection of earrings and necklaces priced less than $20. The sale of these items can definitely add to your total monies at the end of your party.

Like Tupperware, you might want to structure some type of incentive or bonus program for buyers. For example, if someone purchases over $150, you might give him or her a gift certificate with a $10 discount or a free pair of earrings.

Be sure to also reward your hostess/host for giving the party. A fair formula is to offer 10% of the pre-sales tax totals, along with some free jewelry. For parties booked because of the current party, give some type of additional reward. You should also have a pre-structured monetary or jewelry reward if the hostess/host sells over a certain amount at the party. If you structure and compensate your party givers with good awards you can create a structure similar to multi-level programs, where party host/hostesses can recruit and set up their own parties and sell your jewelry for you.

Structuring your incentive program well and making it fun and rewarding can definitely encourage your hostess/host to have another one at a future date. Please don't forget to send a handwritten thank you and mail it right away to show your appreciation.

Most vendors who do home parties use other forms of selling to cross or tie in advertising, like promoting their parties at craft shows. To accomplish this, package your printed literature on your parties and pass them out freely. Include pictures of some of the jewelry you give as rewards to your host/hostess and samples of the invitations you send out. Be sure to include your incentive-payment structures. If you are computer savvy, design a brochure for parties. Be sure to include all the advantages to the hostess/host having the party. Don't forget to list contact information, including your Web site.

KEEPING TRACK OF YOUR INVENTORY AT A HOME PARTY

If you can, bring a friend or relative or hire someone to help you keep an eye on your inventory. They can also help by adding up your sales and wrapping and bagging your jewelry. Having a helper will give you more time to socialize and mingle with guests. Use this time to talk about what inspired you to design certain pieces or why you used the materials you used, or anything related to your designing. Relating to your customers this way will allow your passion to be seen and help your sales tremendously.

To help you keep track of your jewelry, arrange them on an organized display. I'm assuming you would have already worked out what size table your hostess/host will provide or you will bring, so do a detailed layout before your party. Sketch it out on paper with each piece numbered and placed in its exact location. Carry a printout of your layout with you and use it to save time setting up your table and to help you instantly know what items are missing. As you sell pieces, cross them out and you will be able to see what's missing at a glance. It will also help to have all your pieces numbered sequentially on paper and cross them off as they are sold and taken from the display. This way you will have a double check and balance system. You might also like to have some brightly colored preprinted "sold" cut-outs with your numbered jewelry items (you can use paper or sticky labels from an office supply store) so you can stick them on your display, this way you can immediately know what items have been sold. Another method to help keep track of your inventory is to group all like items together (bracelets, necklaces) and number them sequentially.

SPECIAL REQUESTS

More than likely at a home-based party someone will want a custom designed piece or some variation of one of your designs.

For custom orders, be sure both you and the customer have a written and signed copy of what you've agreed to make. I want you to be as detailed as possible, include exact color or design changes. Remember, be exact because after you're in your studio this detailed written order will be all that you have to complete the design. Be sure to write in a delivery date. Don't forget to get their phone number(s) and e-mail address on this form. You may need this if you have any questions or changes with the order. If you want to be totally professional, have a special order form made, you can do it on your computer. Make spaces for the information above and include a blank area for notes or sketches on what the proposed changes will be. One rule you absolutely must stick to when taking custom orders-never ... ever make a firm commitment to a particular style or color of a bead or a variation on a component included in your design unless you are absolutely sure you can get them. Even if you know you can get a particular part of your piece, be realistic on how soon you can have the piece in your possession, especially if you have parts that need to be shipped before you can complete the piece.

CUSTOM JEWELRY - HOW TO MAKE IT YOUR SPECIALTY

Without a doubt, if you are out selling your designs you will be asked to do custom work. Custom orders can be a lucrative and rewarding part of your jewelry design business or it can be your only way of doing business. The most important aspect of doing custom designs is clear and concise communication backed up with exacting paperwork. By following a few simple rules you can create a wonderful reputation as a custom jewelry maker.

Rule 1 - Listen to what your customer wants. Make sure that what they want is a realistic want. Make drawings and discuss what materials they want you to use. Have some examples or items already made up for them to see. Use a color wheel to make sure you have a clear understanding of what colors they want. This can really help because everyone's example of pea green or chartreuse can be different.

Rule 2 – In the initial stages, use your design expertise to add or take away from the proposed design. Again this is when samples or your portfolio of current and/or previous designs can assist you.

Rule 3 – Never give a price quote without knowing precisely what's involved in producing the piece. This includes the materials you will be using and the amount of time required to produce it. You may have to go to extra lengths to get the supplies needed or need more time to make the item you agreed on, so as a safeguard when you give your estimate of charges, add an additional 10% to 20%.

Rule 4 – When your order is an "I needed it yesterday" order, be sure your estimate reflects it. Rush orders can throw you into a scramble to find the right parts, work quickly or take short cuts. If you think a rush order may affect the quality of the piece, it may be better to turn the order down.

Rule 5 – Once you've worked up a quote, put it in writing. Keep it simple and spell out all the particulars. This is one of the most important things you can do to avoid misunderstandings. Your agreement should include:

- All your contact information, along with the current date.
- The customer's contact information, including e-mail address and cell and landline phone numbers (home and work).
- Write a simple description of the piece you plan to do. Again, clearly state what materials you will use. Do a mock sketch, even if you're not an artist. Any crude rendering will do. Having something to refer to for your finished design can help cut down on misunderstandings later. I'm sure you will be asked to design something from a client's broken jewelry. Oftentimes it will have sentimental value to the person, so having clear, concise, written communication between you is absolutely essential.
- Include a statement about any resizing (if applicable), if this can't be determined ahead. This should be done free of charge. Be sure to include in your statement that this does not include any redesigning of the finished piece.
- Ask for at least 50% of the total cost upfront as a nonrefundable deposit, with the balance due upon delivery of the piece. It is extremely important to do this before you order any supplies.

There are lots of reasons why someone would change their mind after commissioning a custom order. Getting half of the total amount beforehand is your guarantee that you will at least be able to cover the cost of your supplies, and some of your time.

- Clearly state the date you expect to finish the jewelry. Again, please allow extra time for unforeseen problems.

- Include a space for the customer's signature and a space for yours. Give your customer a copy of the signed statement and keep a signed one for you.

- When the piece is finished, e-mail a photo/scan to your customer and arrange a pick-up/drop-off date. Be sure to put the piece in a nice jewelry box or pouch.

- After you deliver the custom piece, have the customer sign a simple statement/receipt stating that they have received the piece. You can use a regular two-part receipt book for this, or use your original signed agreement.

- Don't forget to send a thank-you note or an e-mail letting your customer know just how much you appreciate their business.

Inspirational Quote: "Obstacles are those frightful things you see when you take your eyes off your goal," Anonymous.

CHAPTER 9

SELL AT CRAFT SHOWS

Selling at craft shows can be a good way to start out selling your jewelry. Selling this way does require some advance planning. Finding out about events in your area is a good place to start. We've included several sites for you to start with on our resource pages, for more just go online and type "craft show listings" or "art show listings" into your browser. You can also find out about shows in your area by contacting your local chamber of commerce. For more information, please check out our resource pages for their Web site. It will guide you to all the local chamber of commerce organizations throughout the country. On their site, you will be able to type in your city and get all the contact information needed. You can also use this site to access information from your local Convention and Visitors Bureau. This organization is an excellent resource for craft shows. After contacting these organizations, ask if you can be put on their mailing list for upcoming events. Don't overlook your local parks departments as additional sources. Shows provided by any of these organizations usually have nominal fees, so if you're just starting your business, they are ideal. Another plus of participating in inexpensive shows is that they can give you a fair idea of what items sell best for you. Other inexpensive venues to check out include churches and country clubs.

If you don't try some of the venues above, booth prices at professional shows can be expensive and represent quite an investment. Keep in mind that every show is different and what they provide with your booth fee can vary widely. Make sure you read all the fine print when you sign up. Some shows will give you tables; others will require that you bring your own. Most will require that you cover your tables. If you have to cover your own tables, choose a fabric that is lightweight and does not wrinkle easily. Don't forget to ask about chairs so that you can bring one if they are not included in your show fee.

The following rules are ones that I've concluded after selling our vintage beads on the road for several years.

1. Do not attempt to sell your handmade jewelry at low-end swap/flea market type shows. If you decide that this is something you really want to do, make sure you take items that are priced less than $20.

2. Use caution when you sign up for outdoor shows. Usually there's a weather clause in the contract and you absolutely will not get any money back if you are rained or weathered out. I once did an outdoor show in Texas where I flew in from California. It rained ... no, it poured for the entire two days of the show. Since the show was a washout, I had to spread out the money lost over the next few shows.

HOW TO CHOOSE A CRAFT SHOW

❏ There are so many craft/art shows out there. Some of the best shows for crafters are juried. A juried show will require you to send in pictures of your work before you are accepted. Some juried shows may require that you send in pictures or slides of your booth too, so when you do any show take some pictures of your booth and have them on file in case you need them.

❏ Never do a first-time show, but if you do, proceed with caution. New shows take time to build. So, visit the show and put it on your list as a potential venue for another time. Another important thing to remember is that all craft shows are not created equal, you won't get the price you want for your handcrafted items if you are next to someone with imported mass-produced goods. The best advice I can offer on

98

choosing which show to participate in, is to visit the show before you apply for it. Make a potential show file with any pertinent information about the show, along with contact information and future show dates. When visiting the show, pay particular attention and make notes on the following:

❑ The quality of the show, including where it is located.

❑ Is there air conditioning or heat in the venue? I know it might sound unimportant, but ask. Have you ever tried shopping when you are extremely hot or cold? You don't have to answer that one, because I know you won't stay around and shop in extreme temperature conditions if you don't have to, so ask the promoter about the creature comforts.

❑ What kind of people are in attendance? Do they seem to be buying or browsing?

❑ Note the prices of the items being sold, particularly jewelry. Pay close attention to whether there are any niche jewelry areas not being addressed, such as wire-wrapping, pearl-knotting or repair services.

❑ If possible, chat with some of the vendors about the show. If you are visiting near the end of the day, check out the tables and displays for gaps as an indication of how good or bad the show was.

❑ Visit some of the jewelry forums where fellow designers discuss and share their show venues. Refer to our resource pages for a listing of forum URLs.

TIPS ON HOW TO BE A SUCCESS AT A CRAFT SHOW:

✓ Make a check-off list and check it twice. This is very important. If you don't, you will forget something … so just do it! A day or so before the show, pack all your business supplies. Be sure to include your brochures, business cards and receipt books. You should pre-stamp all your invoices with your information or staple a business card to each receipt. Don't forget bags for purchased items, pens, tissue paper, extra blank price tags and a mailing list sign-up sheet. From this sheet you can eventually compile a mailing list so that you can notify customers of upcoming events.

✓ Exactly where is your booth located? Your location in the show is extremely important. If the show layout is broken up with a main room and side rooms or rooms in another part of a building, try to get a space in the main room. Side rooms and illogical booth layouts can be your death at a show.

✓ Make sure you keep good notes on your top buyers, such as what they purchased and why. Take note if their purchase was for their own use or for gift giving.

✓ Remember, presentation is very important. Make sure your booth display is impressive, neat, organized, and that all items can be seen easily. Use risers or covered bricks and boxes to create height on your table. Try thrift shops for unique props for your table displays. If you use showcases, make sure the glass is clean and smudge-free. Cases can add an upscale flair to your booth and can help you get more money for your product. If you need earring/necklace cards, use some nice card stock and decorate them with a rubber stamp. You can also order personalized stamps containing your contact information. Use these to stamp the back of your jewelry cards and any other handouts. Another important tip is to make sure your booth looks abundant. People will interpret a sparse booth as a sign that you are not totally committed. If you don't have enough inventory, team up with another artist to make your presentation look full.

✓ To avoid needless questions, make sure your price tags are easy to read and clearly visible.

✓ Make sure your business cards and brochures are easily accessible to customers and be sure to include one with each purchase.

✓ Make sure your merchant visa signs are easily seen. For detailed information on setting up your account, be sure you read our chapter on the various options for setting up a merchant account. Remember, having a merchant account will increase your sales tremendously.

✓ Make sure you take some sort of wheeled dolly to cart your things to and from your booth; this will save you lots of time and energy. Try Home Depot for options.

✓ Let there be light ... if your show is indoors; make sure you check out how many watts of electrical power you are allowed. Bring extension cords and power strips. More than likely the lighting will be insufficient, so come prepared. Use halogen lights if you can, they duplicate sunlight and will make your jewelry twinkle. Shine bright and your sales will increase.

✓ Don't forget the duct tape. You will find yourself using this for all sorts of things, like taping your power cords securely to the floor to avoid tripping.

✓ Please bring some kind of sign or banner if the show doesn't provide one. Missing that one customer because they didn't see you is not something you want to happen.

✓ Bring your jewelry tools and your stringing supplies with you, just in case you need to do some last minute repairs.

✓ Bring help, if possible. Keeping an eye on your booth and making a sell at the same time is practically impossible to do.

✓ Stand, please - at your booth, that is. Sitting behind your booth is rude and self-defeating. Customers won't search you out. Stay standing and be ready with a smile and information about your jewelry. Be informative and educate your customers on what materials you used and perhaps a bit about how you designed your pieces, but no "Chatty Cathy's" please.

✓ Don't forget your change. A few days before the show get at least $100 in assorted bills and loose change.

✓ No one knows your jewelry like you do, so even if you bring an assistant, don't leave him or her to sell for you as you wander around the show. Keep in mind that you are there to sell your items, not to have a good time visiting other vendors.

Although craft fairs are a great way to sell, there are hundreds of other places where you can sell your jewelry. Sometimes doing events that are not jewelry related can make your work stand out. Use the following list as a loose guide:

- Baby's, children's expo (do some pieces with a baby theme.)

- Gems, jewelry & lapidary shows

- Garden shows (make some items with a floral theme using leaves and flowers.)

- Bridal & Wedding shows

- Antique shows (particularly if your designs have a vintage feel.)

- Fashion shows

- Hotel & Resort shows

- Pet shows: horse, bird, cat, or dog shows (make pet jewelry your niche market)

- Religious expos (use religious charms.)

- Motorcycle rallies

- Car club shows

Any of the above events could be very profitable for you. To find out about events like these, do your homework and locate clubs, groups or organizations that host these events.

Having your jewelry in a venue that may not customarily have jewelry could work to your advantage. Designing a few items geared toward the organization or group can only help. You might also try local businesses for their in-house sales events. Businesses are always trying to think of clever promotional items to give to their special customers. Why not design some simple earrings using miniature teapots for a local teashop or make wine-charm earrings for a local winery, wine club or store. Use some bridge charms for your local bridge club or some little gardening charms for a garden club.

Selling any of the above ways can be fun and easy, but remember it does require quite a bit of physical labor, like getting your items to and from your booth, setting up your display and keeping it in order throughout the day. If you are not used to it, being on your feet all day can add to your exhaustion, but the smile on your face after a successful show can easily make up for it.

One last note-enjoy your event, pay attention to both your booth and your customers and make notes on any feedback you get.

Once the show is over, do a full evaluation of it. Put your conclusions into your file; you can refer to it to help determine whether or not you want to participate in it again.

ৡৢৡৢৡৢৡৢৡৢ

Inspirational Quote: "To accomplish great things, we must not only act, but also dream; not only plan, but also believe," Anatole France.

CHAPTER 10

WHOLESALING:

SELL DIRECT TO SPECIALTY BOUTIQUES/GALLERIES YOURSELF OR HAVE A FRIEND DO IT FOR YOU!

If you are serious about turning you passion into money, you can approach consignment stores, clothing stores, galleries or other shops where your jewelry will fit in. This will require a serious commitment on your part, but doing so can aid you in developing profitable business relationships with merchants. Selling direct to specialty stores can help you quickly build up clientele and can be very lucrative. If you are committed to selling this way, there is one cardinal rule that you should follow no matter what type of store/boutique you sell to, and that is, "never compete with them." This simply means that you should either have a wholesale line that is different from your retail line so that if you sell at surrounding shows you won't be competing with your wholesale accounts. You might also have a wholesale and a retail line that is at different price points. If you do choose to retail and wholesale the same items, make sure your retail prices are the same or above the prices your retail accounts sell at. By paying attention to all the fine points you can combine these two ways of selling. Having wholesale accounts can even out low sale craft shows, low Internet sales or whatever other ways you sell and give you more financial stability.

Wholesaling your work can be difficult or it can be easy once you know a few tricks of the trade. If you live in a sparsely populated area or need to spend more time at home instead of doing craft shows every weekend, wholesale accounts can work to your advantage. When I first started my jewelry business, I depended on a few wholesale accounts to guide me through the rough spots by giving me enough predictability to pay my bills. Please don't be nervous about approaching shops and galleries. Remember they need you to. They are not doing you a favor by accepting your jewelry, if you approach them with that attitude, they will definitely pick up on it and it won't work to your advantage. Keep in mind that you are offering them a unique line of jewelry that their customers won't find in other shops in the area. Besides, most shop owners are constantly on the lookout for new and different merchandise. They also need suppliers (including jewelry artists) who are reliable and professional to do business with.

Before you head out and knock on doors, do your homework. Walk or drive in an area you want to sell in. Write down store names and addresses. If the store is open, go inside and browse, make a note of what the average price points are (the range of prices from high to low). Try to determine if your wholesale and retail prices fall within the price range of the average number of accessories. Notice what lines of merchandise they carry, and how they are displayed. Pay special attention to their jewelry lines. Is it mostly a particular style, like Art Nouveau or youthful contemporary? What's on the tags, are there prices only or do the tags carry information about the item? Do they have too much jewelry already? How would your jewelry fit? Could your designs stand out among the competition? You should also key in on the character, atmosphere and direction of the store to determine if your designs will fit. When you get back to your car, jot down the key points you took in while in the store, this will help you later when you make the final decision on which stores to call on.

If the shop has a Web site, browse through it. Read all the text and examine all the photos closely. Check for as many of the previously mentioned points as you can online.

While in the store get a business card, or get the telephone number from the telephone directory or online later. When you are ready to telephone the store, work out your marketing technique to get an appointment.

You will more than likely get someone who answers the phone who is not the owner, so they are screening the calls. If they tell you the buyer is not in ask them when would be a good time to call back. With persistence you will more than likely get through to the buyer or owner, so have your script well rehearsed. Practice it with friends and family or in front of a mirror or into a tape recorder. Don't memorize what you want to say, but get comfortable with it so that your delivery will be natural, not forced or robotic. Over time and with experience you will be able to adjust your responses to the person on the other end of the phone.

SETTING UP AN APPOINTMENT

The following are examples of what you might say:

"Is the buyer in? (you)

May I ask who is calling? (store)

This is Susie Edwards. (you)

Susie, what is this about? (store)

I represent a fabulous jewelry collection that I know would be a great addition to your store. (you)

Susie, thank you for your call; however, we are not necessarily looking for new designers right now. (store)

I can appreciate that, in fact I was in your store a few days ago, and I was impressed with the lines you already carry, however, my line is completely different from what you have already and I know it would sell extremely well in your store. (you)

What kind of price points do you have? (store)

We have excellent price points, and they are definitely within your price range. What day would be good for you to take a quick look at some pieces? I won't take much of your time and of course there is no obligation to buy. I know you will be extremely pleased." (you)

TIP: *Note the choice of words I used like, "take a quick look" and the conclusions I made, leaving them with the final decision of choosing what day would be good for them.*

At this point, the store buyer may ask for more details, so be prepared to tell the buyer about your line. I've found from experience it's better to say you represent the line you're selling, even if you are the designer and the manufacturer. You will seem more professional, and you won't be subjected to discounting on the spot, or providing personal favors. Once you have an appointment, call the day before to reconfirm. Be on time for your appointment! But don't be too early either; arriving 30 minutes or earlier can be just as unprofessional as being late. Make sure all your samples are well organized and tagged with prices and style numbers. Once you have an order, be sure to write them neatly and make sure you note any detailed changes to be done on the order. If your appointment is during business hours, be prepared for interruptions. Plan on the appointment lasting at least an hour.

If a shop owner declines to make an appointment with you because they "already have enough jewelry" or some other reason, don't take it personally or feel stressed about it. Just let that one go and contact the next one on your list. Sometimes it's just the wrong time of year for the shop to buy, or their sales may be slow or finances tight. Try to leave a door open, ask if you can call or send an e-mail periodically to check whether there's anything they'd like to order from you.

Never...ever just drop by a shop with your jewelry. Shop owners appreciate it when artists make an appointment to see them, rather than just waltzing in off the street, expecting them to be idle. Shop owners are extremely busy with the day-to-day tasks of running a business and find it annoying when artists don't understand their busy schedules. Trust me, dropping in won't get you off on the right foot.

MORE QUESTIONS YOU COULD BE ASKED:

1. Will you buy back the items that don't sell? It's your call but think about this one long and hard, you don't want to be taken advantage of. I would proceed with caution on this.

2. Do you offer a discount for volume buying? If you do, have a discount schedule printed and available. If you don't, you might respond by saying "because your prices are very competitive, other wholesale accounts have found your price points more than adequate for a good profit margin."

3. Do you also sell your jewelry at retail? This simply means do you sell your items at craft shows etc. The reason the store is asking you this is because they don't want you competing with them at cheaper prices. It is important to let them know that you will not undersell them, that your retail prices are priced at or above what they will be selling your items for.

4. How much time do you need for a special request? The amount of time you take to produce an order may be important if the store needs a special order. Tell them that because each special request is different it's impossible to give an exact amount of time, but that you always work as efficiently as you can to expedite a request.

5. How long have you been in business? Be honest on this one, if you've been making jewelry for a year but selling for six months, say so. Inexperience, could or could not work in your favor, usually it works against you.

WHAT TO EXPECT AFTER YOUR APPOINTMENT IS SET:

- The shop owner who wants everything at reduced prices and will complain about everything. They will continually ask you for extras and will generally want you to perform some task every time they see you. Even when your designs sell well, they will need or want something beyond what you usually provide to your wholesale accounts. If this happens to you, don't hesitate to inform them that although you appreciate and value their business, because of tight time constraints you won't be able to perform whatever the task they request. If they persist, "stop doing business with them." Trust me, in the long run you will be happy that you did. This type of buyer is probably like that about most things and will never be satisfied no matter how many hoops you jump through. Remember, playing to their tune cannot only affect your creative flow, but the bottom line....your bank account.

- The upper-end arrogant type store or gallery. Oftentimes this type of buyer may love your designs, but may try to make you feel inadequate or inferior so that you can give them better prices or even consignment. Don't let this type of buyer intimidate you. They are relying on the fact that you really want your jewelry in their shop and are probably in the habit of using artists' inventories to stock their shelves. Don't buy the hype, stand your ground and treat them as you would any other buyer.

- The shop owner who wants you to bill them later. They will give you the usual info on how their accountant pays their vendors every 30 days and it's the only way they can do business with you. If they paid you in 30 days, I'm sure you would be able to handle the wait, but at least 90% of the time you won't receive your money in 30 days. This may not mean that they are a bad account, but at least if you know going into it that you probably won't get your money within thirty days, you won't be expecting it. Ask if they have a Dunn & Bradstreet rating and tell them that your business manager requires it before extending credit. Remember it takes time to build trust. If you do decide to provide a new account with terms, start out low, extending only the amount of credit you feel comfortable giving. I recommend $300 or less. If you've extended credit and the account is overdue, don't be afraid to call up and ask for your money. After you've heard a couple of excuses on why you haven't received your money, accept them and call again in a couple of weeks. After two months/60 days, your relationship is over. Return to the shop to get your jewelry back. This is where all the detailed paperwork (itemizing the exact pieces with colors, etc.) you gave them when you sold the pieces will come in handy. Besides, if you end up in small claims court, it's the only way you can win the case. In the beginning of my business, I would have my husband handle all my collections. It made me seem more professional and he was more objective, since he wasn't as emotionally involved. He handled one interesting collection problem. We had a 90-day past-due account with a very high-end group of stores. These stores were located in prestigious areas in California. After being on the telephone with their accounting department for more than three months, he was absolutely sick of hearing excuses and threatened that we would carry picket signs in front of their flagship store in Beverly Hills stating that they did not pay their vendors. That's all it took, our check was immediately cut, and we had it in our hands in less than six hours..Funny how exposure and the threat of embarrassment got us what we wanted immediately. The moral of the story is no matter how upper-end or well-heeled a store appears, if they don't pay you, what difference does it make. Pull out all your antennas when it comes to extending credit, if you feel uncomfortable or can't afford to do it, tell them. A great alternative with someone who insists on credit is to tell him or her that you can supply them with the jewelry, but with first orders you do require a credit card number to hold. If you receive the check in 30 days, you won't charge their card. To make the deal even better, tell them that you can offer them 60 days without payment with a credit card number. Who would pass up a 60-day arrangement? If they do, pass on them. It's a good sign that they probably have no intention of paying you and you will be saving yourself a lot of future problems.

- The store whose inventory looks sparse or not cared for. This store may be on the way out. If they are, and they ask for consignment or net-30 payments and you agree, you may be sorry. Be cautious and let your intuitive sense guide you.

DRESS TO IMPRESS FOR YOUR APPOINTMENT

Dress nicely. A pair of nice comfortable slacks with a matching top will do. Don't forget to wear your own jewelry; but don't overdo it. Use a professional portable jewelry display for carrying and displaying your items.

Invest in a couple of jewelry display trays or cases. They don't need to be expensive. There are plenty of inexpensive jewelry folders and rolls including bracelet and necklace rolls. There are also sample trays/cases with clear see-thru tops. Any of these are excellent ways to present your line with professional flair.

Be sure to have your business cards, price lists, order forms (with duplicates), copies of your artist statement or bio, and any information with photos or color scans of your jewelry in a folder, briefcase, or pocket in your jewelry display case. Have some pens for filling out your order forms and don't forget your calculator.

TIP: If you have invested in color brochures, postcards or photo sheets, be sure the prices aren't printed on them because if you ever need to lower or raise your prices you won't have to reproduce the whole sheet. Print a separate price list that you can attach to your photos.

DURING YOUR APPOINTMENT

Be enthusiastic and knowledgeable about your work. Talk about the kind of stones, or beads you've used in your pieces. Share only tidbits of the process you used to create them. Don't bore your potential buyer with long drawn-out details on how you created each and every piece. Remember, your goal is to sell your items not to teach them your process.

Be sure to ask if they have any special requirements for the labeling or packaging of your jewelry. Most shops don't want information about you on their tags. However, they will appreciate tags with information about the items you used in the piece. If it's not clear what you should or should not include, just ask.

If you do include detailed tags of the materials used in your items, mention that their sales associates can use your personalized tags to assist them in pointing out how special and original your pieces are.

Sometimes a shop may want gift boxes, pouches, etc. to be sold with your pieces. Even if they don't, figure in the cost of boxes/pouches when you calculate your wholesale prices. Do some homework and find a good wholesale jewelry box supplier. Use your browser again by going online and entering "wholesale jewelry box supplier."

AFTER YOUR APPOINTMENT

After your appointment, send a hand-written thank-you note. Thank them for taking the time to look at your pieces. Do this even if they didn't buy from you. Sending a thank you will definitely leave a good and lasting impression, and may make it easier for you to approach the store at a later date or when you change your style, if that was the reason they didn't buy.

If you don't land an order, offer to do a trunk show for them.

SETTING UP A TRUNK SHOW

There are many reasons why a store may not want to purchase your jewelry and it may not be personal. Your timing could be off, they may have just purchased product or reached their allotted budget for the month or quarter. They may think their store has enough jewelry, even if they adore yours. If you can't land a sale, offer to do a trunk show for them. Because they have nothing to lose and profit to gain, they may jump at the chance. You might consider working a trunk show in before one of the major holidays, like Christmas, Mother's day or Easter.

Tell them you can provide your own table and display, either inside the store or directly in front of it. Come up with a workable percentage of the sales and run all transactions through their cash register. For this, you should have a three-part receipt book. One receipt will be for you, one will be for the store, and one will be for the customer. The purchases chosen at your display should be totaled with one receipt stapled to the customer's bag and one handed over to the store cashier. At the end of the day your numbered receipts and the store's receipts should match. This will make it easy to figure out the prearranged percentages.

Make sure your display table is attractive; a floor-length tablecloth will make your display look nice and hide any items you may want to keep out of sight.

Ask the business owner to e-mail or distribute flyers to all their customers with the date and time of your show. If time doesn't allow them to do so, tell them you can help with it.

Remember the type of business you approach to do a trunk show doesn't necessarily have to be a jewelry or clothing boutique, however it might help to somehow tie your jewelry into whatever the primary focus of the shop may be. A good friend of mind had a great trunk show at a very high-end wine store. They were having a wine tasting and she made several wire-twisted jewelry pieces using amethyst beads to form what looked like grapes on a vine. Needless to say, she sold out at the wine tasting and gained a list of very high-end potential customers…so keep your mind open and you will be able to come up with all kinds of unconventional potential venues.

If your sales are a success at the store's event, they will always remember you; and more than likely they will be willing to give you an encore performance. That point made, another one is that almost all shop owners will be willing to purchase some of your items after they have had their customers compliment you and them and buy your jewelry.

AFTER YOU LAND THE ACCOUNT/OR GET A TRUNKSHOW

If you get a store account in a particular area, don't sell to their competitors a few blocks down. It's called respecting territories, and selling the same thing to the store in the next block is not smart business.... Establish some boundaries, please.

Again, after you have a trunk show, or land an account, stay in touch with the shop owners. Practice some restraint, don't contact them so often that you become annoying. A few well-timed e-mails or phone calls should do the trick. If you are considerate and thoughtful your jewelry business will thrive and prosper and you will develop a solid personal relationship with the people you do business with.

Remember the relationship between you and the shop owner is a business marriage and you must get along and understand each other's needs or it just won't work.

❧❧❧❧❧❧❧❧❧❧

Inspirational Quote "The secret to happiness is not in doing what one likes to do, but in liking what one has to do," Anonymous.

CHAPTER 11

CONSIGNMENT – THE BIG "C" WORD

Without a doubt if you approach stores with your jewelry to sell, you will be asked to place them on consignment. I'm sure anyone reading this book already knows the correct definition of Consignment, but for those who don't, consignment is when you leave your designs at a store with no monetary exchange. You are paid a predetermined percentage if and when the store sells your designs.

Before considering consignment, read the following chapter and keep in mind some of the important points we will cover.

In my years of designing, my only consignment deal was not a good experience. After much insistence from one of my reps I accepted a deal with a major, prestigious chain. They would only work with new accessory designers on a consignment basis. My rep insisted that once my items sold, the chain would then place a net-30 order. Once my accessories were placed in the store, they all sold in two or three weeks. The store immediately wanted to place another consignment order with my rep, without paying for the previous shipment. I refused to do another order until the outstanding invoice was paid in full. Several weeks later, I received a partial check for less than half of the items I had shipped. For the next several months, each time I received a payment, it was for only a few items. This process went on for more than a year with small checks dribbling in. I felt used. This store truly had the money and prestige to pay their small vendors but chose instead to use them. This kind of consignment deal still exists today. Even small boutiques will use your inventory to fill their store, and even though it may sell out quickly, some will choose not to pay you until they want to. I believe this is called, "rob Peter to pay Paul."

With this said, when making a decision to place your items in a shop, you should do a thorough analysis on why you think the establishment would want your items without paying for them. Read between the lines, they could be saying:

1) "I don't make enough money to buy your jewelry but I need or want it in my shop."

2) "I have poor cash flow right now."

3) "I may be out of business soon." The possibility exists that the shop may be in financial trouble and that they can't or won't pay you your percentage of the sale, no matter how good their intentions are.

4) "I like your work, but I'm not sure it would sell in my store."

Even if you can't sense any of the things above and all signs point to the shop being well-run, remember you are still entrusting the maintenance, care, and method of selling of your product to them. At the risk of sounding redundant I have to say again, pay attention to how organized the shop is. You don't need the additional headache of a shop that is poorly managed.

Remember these strong disadvantages before consigning:

❑ More than likely you will have a lag in time between delivering your jewelry and when you get your money after your item sells. So be prepared to have a backup cash flow. I would not recommend this route if you have cash flow problems already.

❑ You will definitely have to maintain very detailed records of items left on consignment. So be prepared to spend a considerable amount of time with documentation and paperwork.

❑ There is a possibility that your pieces may be lost, stolen or damaged before they are sold. This is why it is very important to pay attention to how organized the store is.

- There is a possibility that the shop may not be as motivated to sell your items because they haven't invested any money in them.

Consigning does have some advantages, including the following:

- You can have numerous venues selling your work without your presence. If you've included contact information on your jewelry display cards, it could work to your advantage by providing free advertising.

- Unlike production work, you will have the freedom to produce your items without deadlines.

- It's much easier to get your items into a shop on consignment.

- You can use your consignment accounts to test-market new designs.

If after reading the information above you've made the decision to do consignment, please follow the steps below on protecting your jewelry. Remember that until it's sold, you still own it; so don't be careless about protecting your property. Keeping accurate documentation is the key to protecting your investment. Keep a detailed record of each piece of jewelry; include the style number, the color, and the kind of beads used in the piece. An example of a detailed consignment item should look like the chart on the next page.

Detailed record of item left on consignment.	
Style Number	1005
Item consigned	Chandelier Earrings-1 pair
Materials used in this item	Sterling Silver Chain, 5301-6mm-Siam Swarovski Crystals-12pc, Crystal Rondell spacers –6pcs
Photo attached	Yes
Store/gallery that received this item	The Luna Gallery
Date received	01-04-00
Agreed selling price	$85.00
Percentage of this item	60/40
Length of time item will be consigned	3 months from date above 03-04-00

Well-run shops and galleries will send you a monthly or quarterly sales report. Be sure to check it against your own records to be sure all your pieces have been accounted for. If the shop doesn't send you a report, send one to them; doing so will help keep your accounting and your consigned items in their minds.

LETS TALK ABOUT PERCENTAGES

The most common consignment percentage is 60/40. This simply means that 60% of the money from the sale of your jewelry will go to you and 40% will go to the shop. This is the typical percentage arrangement, but depending on the shop, the consignment percentage can vary from as low as

50/50, where you and the shop split the proceeds of the sale equally or as high as 80/20 - 80% to you and 20% to the shop.

Never go any lower than 60/40, accepting a 50/50 consignment percentage is truly unfair to you as an artist and as a businessperson. Getting a larger percentage will help you because you are taking a risk with your jewelry items and should be compensated for it. Besides, you will need the extra percentage to compensate for the increased amount of paperwork and documentation you will have to do. Keep in mind that consigning is a risky arrangement for you because your inventory will be out of circulation while it's on display in the shop, so your cash flow for those items will be tied up until they sell them. Remember having a consignment contract is like making an investment in another person's business. By arranging for a percentage not lower than 60/40 you will at least be able to recoup on your investment when you finally get the check in the mail for items sold.

LET'S TALK ABOUT YOUR PHOTOS - THE ONLY WAY TO DOCUMENT!!

Use any method you want to take pictures of your consigned inventory. I love using my computer scanner since the lighting is already perfect and the set-up is simple and quick. It literally takes minutes to lay out your pieces on the scanner surface. Use your editing software to tweak whatever area you think needs it. Of course you can use a digital camera or regular film camera but I prefer scanner photos. Whatever method you use, keep the pictures, along with style numbers and any other consignment information on each shop in a separate folder. An extra benefit of having photos attached with style numbers is that you will have all the information in one place if a customer requests a special order. Documenting with photos is very important. Make sure in your consignment invoice you leave an area showing that you have included a photo; this should be labeled as an addendum on your consignment invoice.

YOU CAN CREATE YOUR OWN CONSIGNMENT CONTRACT OR USE OUR SAMPLE.

You should include a consignment contract with each collection of jewelry you deliver to a shop. Again, keep a copy of this contract in the file you created for each store. I created my own contract on the computer and you can do the same, but if you prefer you can access a PDF blank contract form on our Web site at www.pudgypublishing.com. A filled in sample consignment contract can be viewed in the back of this book.

When creating your own contract, be sure to include:

1. Your business name, address and all contact information.

2. The actual date the consignment started and the date it will end, if the items are not sold.

3. The shop name and contact information. If the contact person is different from the owner, be sure to include that persons name along with the owner's/manager's full name.

4. The shop's resale tax number or business license. At the end of the year, you will need this information to show that the shop-not you-is responsible for the sales tax of the items sold on your behalf.

5. The description and quantity of any displays you have your items displayed on.

6. The style numbers of all the items left for consignment on your master invoice. Be sure to add an addendum after the style numbers indicating that you've included a detailed record of each item along with photos that are attached to the record.

7. Leave a space at the bottom for your signature, along with the shop owner's/manager's signature.

8. Include a space for information on when and how the shop will pay you for sold items.

9. Be sure to include a space for information on returning any unsold items to you ... mainly how, and if applicable, who will pay for the return. If your items need to be shipped to return them, spell it out in your contract so you will know which party will pay for shipping.

KEEPING IN TOUCH WITH YOUR CONSIGNED INVENTORY

Keeping in touch with each shop you consign your jewelry in will help keep losses at a minimum and definitely aid in making the chances of your consignment venture a success.

Keeping track of the sales activity at each shop is crucial. Use your computer and make up a sales activity sheet. Have a section for each style number and the date it sold. Keep your eyes open for any patterns in your sales activity. From your sales activity sheet you should be able to see what your best sellers are. Keeping up with what items sell will help you with restocking, so that your inventory is always fresh and replenished. Remember to send your shop a monthly or six-week update of this activity sheet, if they don't send you one.

Keeping your sales activity records up will also help you instantly see which shops are working for you and which ones are not. Once you are armed with this information you will be able to decide whether to take a different approach. That could include changing the style of inventory you placed in that particular shop or ending your relationship with them.

Another important attribute of your sales activity sheet is that it will aid you in seeing if your consigned inventory items turn up missing. Using this form diligently will definitely help you track down missing inventory in a timely manner and minimize your losses.

Overall, consignment selling will mean more work on your part, because it involves more record keeping than other ways of selling your jewelry. Remember the major plus with consigning is that you increase your chances of getting into shops that you might not ordinarily be able to get into.

If you take a responsible professional approach with your record keeping, you can forge a good working relationship with shop owners and win by building your reputation and your jewelry accounts.

IF IT'S CONSIGNMENT FOR YOU, THINGS TO REMEMBER:

- Check out the shop carefully before approaching them about consigning your items.

- Pay close attention to what kind of care they appear to give to the merchandise that's already in their shop.

- Does the shop's overall appearance appear to be in good order and well cared for?

- Will your items be unique in the store or do they already have items that resemble your work?

- Remember to stick with only proven shops that have been in business for several years, or consign a small amount of jewelry in a new store that hasn't had a chance to prove itself yet.

- Start with just a few pieces until you feel confident that your consignment relationship will be successful. Remember, it's not a good idea to start out by consigning more jewelry than you can afford to lose.

- Keep in close touch with the consignment shop once you've delivered your jewelry. If it's close by, stop in occasionally to check on your jewelry and get feedback. Pay attention to the condition it's in, and with where and how it's being displayed. If your shop/gallery is in another town, call or e-mail frequently to check on things.

- Set a specific time limit for the shop or gallery to sell your jewelry, and state it in your consignment agreement. If your work hasn't sold within that time frame, arrange to have it returned to you. It doesn't make financial sense to let your inventory sit any longer than necessary without earning you a return on your investment.

- Be sure to ask if insurance is provided by the shop for jewelry consigned. Ask for details on theft or loss coverage.

- Be sure to ask when and how often they will pay you and if a statement of the jewelry sold will be included with your payment.

- What method will the shop use for returning any unsold items to you?

- FYI, many states have consignment laws to protect artists. Since each state and the laws that govern them are different, if you are interested go online and type in your state and the words "consignment laws" and you should be able to get some information that will assist you.

- Don't forget the ever-important signatures, at the bottom of your consignment invoice; be sure there are duplicate copies for each party's records.

- If you provide jewelry displays, don't forget to include photos of them with your contract. Make sure you add this to your original contract as a signed addendum.

  ✓ **Tip:** *If you are truly interested in leaving some of your items on consignment, try high-end clothing consignment stores, instead of jewelry or accessory stores, you'll have less competition and your jewelry can be coordinated with the clothing for major impact and major selling.*

125

✓ **Tip**: *Having your items consigned in a high end well established shop could work to your advantage if you use them as a calling card to help you secure other accounts.*

✓ **Tip:** *Be sure to study our consignment contract at the end of this book. Remember, if you need a blank contract you can download it from our Web site at www.pudgypublishing.com.*

SUMMING IT ALL UP

As you can see, consigning will require a tremendous amount of paperwork. Even if you adore the little shop and find that you and the owner have lots in common, don't take unnecessary risks with your items and skip on any of the paperwork ...after all, business is business. Don't let anything sway you from adequate compensation, work with the numbers and arrive at a profitable, fair percentage for you and the shop owner. Besides an honest, financially stable shop owner who really likes your jewelry will want to have a good long lasting relationship with you. Remember that your goal is to maximize your profits and minimize your losses ... good luck!

ೋ∼ಲ∽∼ಲ∽∼ಲ∽∼ಲ∽∼ಲ

Inspirational Quote: "Yesterday is but a dream, and tomorrow is only a vision, but today well-lived makes every yesterday a dream of happiness and every tomorrow a vision of hope." Anonymous.

CHAPTER 12

FOUR OTHER WAYS TO SELL

FUNDRAISER, CORPORATE, PUSHCART, CRAFT MALLS

FUNDRAISER SALES

Utilizing charities to sell your jewelry is a wonderful way to sell. Non-profit organizations come in many colors, including community service programs, religious institutions, or even a race for a specific cause. All these non-profits are limited in how much money they can earn and still remain a non-profit organization. Although they are limited in their earnings, they have no restrictions in how much money they can bring in through donations. Any organization you choose is more than happy to receive donations of both money and merchandise. This is one of my favorite ways of selling because it cannot only link you to a specific cause but can reward your business financially and provide you with a way to grow your mailing database for future craft shows or home parties. A good place to start is by contacting any hospital, church, homeless shelter or nonprofit organization you feel kindred to. Oftentimes people simply choose a charity they have a personal connection with. I'm sure some cause or concern has more than likely touched your life, your family, or your friends in some way. You may even have been encouraged, enlightened, nurtured, or strengthened by such an organization. Whatever your reasons, if you choose a cause that you are genuinely passionate about your true enthusiasm will shine through.

Another benefit to both you and the charity you choose is that people purchasing from you will feel good knowing that they are not only getting beautiful handmade jewelry, but that part of the purchase price is going to a good cause.

Supporting a charity this way can be an opportunity for your jewelry and you to:

- Have your name and jewelry aligned with a positive humanitarian cause. It can allow you to connect with peers who share similar interest and passion.

- Show your current and future customers that you are not just interested in selling your jewelry, but you also care about supporting and helping people.

- Provide you with free advertising. This can be invaluable; word of mouth advertising is absolutely the best kind of advertising there is.

There are three ways to contribute to your chosen organization. The first way is by simply contributing pieces of your jewelry to an already existing fundraising event. Oftentimes, it's an auction, although it could be a bazaar or a banquet with an auction. Auction fundraisers always print a pre-auction listing with the items for sale along with the name and address of the company donating them. During the auction preview, when the items are on display, your business cards and/or fliers should be along side them. This type of advertising can benefit your business enormously.

If this is the method you choose, make sure all your items are clearly marked with all pertinent contact information, phone numbers, Web site, etc. A major benefit of contributing your jewelry this way is that it's a great way to build future customers who may either purchase from you or contact you for other fundraising events.

The second way you can contribute is by including "awareness jewelry," in your existing line of jewelry. If you already sell at shows or home parties, you can devote a small portion of your table space for your "awareness jewelry." Make sure you have contacted and received an okay from the organization you plan on donating to. You can decide if you want to contribute a percentage or the whole amount of your chosen items to the organization. There are specific colors that represent several organizations and illnesses. For a list of awareness colors, check out the listing on our resource page.

The third way you can contribute is by organizing an event of your own. You can do this solo or with the organization's assistance. Organizing a jewelry-show fundraiser for your favorite charity can be fun and profitable, especially if you have good organizational skills. Your event can be a silent auction or any other interesting event you can think of. You can even invite other designers to participate; doing so can help make your event well-rounded.

Getting attendance for your fundraiser is a very important part of making it a success. Deciding who will be responsible for advertising is something that should be discussed early on; oftentimes it's both parties. Ask your chosen organization to help. Perhaps they have a newsletter or an employee who can make sure everyone is notified. They might even have a mailing list they can provide you with from previous fundraisers. If your event will have a co-op of vendors, you can require each of them to contribute to the attendance by mailing out invitations from their personal mailing list. Make up flyers, invitations or postcards to advertise the event. If you are computer savvy you can design them, if not solicit someone to donate their services for the fundraiser by designing a nice promotional piece. You might suggest to your organization that you are willing to be in charge of designing the flyer/invitation (with their approval) and they can be in charge of printing and distributing them.

Getting a press release to your local newspaper with all the details of your fundraiser is important. The guidelines for getting your press release to the right person will more than likely require a little research on your part, but the results will be well worth the effort.

Having a small budget for help with advertising is something that you should have discussed in your original proposal to the organization, with everything spelled out clearly.

Deciding where the event will take place is another issue that should be discussed early on. The organization may be able to provide a banquet room, an employee cafeteria or a conference room. You might be able to have the event at your home. Consider a spring garden party. Better yet, you may be able to get a restaurant or a hotel to donate a room. Again, be sure to write all the fine points out in your agreement/proposal. Simply make an outline with all the details and expectations of each party. Don't forget to leave a space for both signatures.

Immediately after your event, hand-deliver your donation check, along with a hand-written thank you to the person at the organization who helped you. Let them know you will definitely be interested in doing future fundraiser jewelry events for them. For tax purposes, be sure to get a receipt for your donation check. After all, in the taxman's book, it's a write-off for your business.

All-in-all, fundraiser jewelry shows can be a great source of money for you. Aligning yourself with an organization can give your jewelry business positive publicity and a database of potential customers.

CORPORATE SELLING

I won't spend a lot of time on this method of selling, but I want you to know that it can be very profitable, without any of the incumbent disadvantages. I have a jewelry-designer friend who lives on the East Coast and flies to Southern California twice a year, usually before major holidays. She schedules a lunchtime jewelry show at a prominent law firm in a prestigious area of Los Angeles that has more than 100 female attorneys and paralegals. Her regular selling ventures have become something that her customers look forward to and so does she. She sells enough jewelry to make her trip very profitable. It's not uncommon for her to make more than $8,000 in half a day during one of her scheduled events. Having access to a company like this can definitely help you sell your jewelry. If you don't have a personal in, try creating one by researching companies online. Do a search for women-owned businesses. You will come up with some interesting and varied companies to start your marketing research for possible clients. One positive plus is that once you have a couple of clients inside a major corporation wearing your creations, they will be asked where they got their jewelry from. So have your Web site up and running so that you can gain new customers without even trying.

If you don't work in this kind of environment, don't know an office manager or don't have a friend who works in a large company, resort to what will always work-cold calling. Don't get discouraged. It may take some time to reach the right person and to find a company willing to listen, but persistence will pay off. Have your pitch perfected, with information you've put together especially for corporate selling, so when you find the right person, you will be prepared. Also be prepared to forward any printed promotional information you have on your company. You will be surprised at the great results you can get. Sometimes they will even print your appointment in the company newsletter for extra advertising. Design a tasteful flyer on nice stationary with details about you and what you are selling. If you've aligned yourself with a charitable organization, be sure to include details about this so they will know that they are getting beautiful jewelry along with contributing to a cause. This can be a very profitable way to sell with very few expenses on your part. Once you've lined up your companies and had one event, try to schedule a return performance. If it was a success, you can be on your way to having a steady income and a great venue for selling your jewelry.

PUSHCART SELLING

You see them everywhere, pushcarts or freestanding kiosks. You will find them strategically placed in malls, at farmers markets and in front of shops. Besides investing in your jewelry, selling from a pushcart can represent a sizeable investment on your part. The average cart can cost a minimum of $2,000 to a maximum of $20,000. Whether you purchase your cart or lease it, prices will vary greatly, depending on where your pushcart is located. If it is in a major, high-traffic or prestigious mall, you will pay more. If you are selling at a farmers market or at a lower-end chain store, the costs can be substantially less. At a boutique that I frequent, I chatted with a jewelry-pushcart owner who purchased her own cart and made a deal with the shop to sell, using the trunk-show method on weekends and during major holidays. The boutique wanted the vendor, but had no space inside of her already heavily stocked shop; so by providing her own pushcart, the jewelry artist was able to sell and make a great profit. If you decide to invest in your own pushcart, remember that there are all kind of venues in which to sell at, including show/expo events in your local area.

Some malls allow pushcart selling on a seasonal basis, with the space being leased for a particular allotted time. Before you get committed to a pushcart arrangement, make sure you do some homework. Visit the mall at peak and non-peak times, and snoop around. Talk to some of the smaller merchants in the mall you are considering to find out what kind of people shop there. Are they mostly young people, middle-aged or families? How long have most of the carts been there? Is there much turnover? Is the mall in a high, middle, or lower income area? These points are extremely important because they will help you determine if your jewelry price points are right for the area.

Try to make sure that mall management isn't using pushcarts as a source of income because they need it as a way to keep them viable and in business. This is important because it can affect your success in a negative or positive way.

CRAFT MALLS

Craft malls allow you to rent space on a month-to-month basis. Oftentimes craft malls are combined with antique/collectible marts. As a jewelry maker, you will typically rent a showcase or shelf space. The price for rentals varies depending on where the mall is located, where you are located within the mall and how much traffic the mall gets. You are responsible for stocking and displaying your items. The mall is responsible for selling the merchandise. If the mall takes a commission, it is typically a very small one. Sometimes you are required to share floor time with other vendors to assist customers as they shop. This may be anywhere from a few hours to a few days per month.

You've heard this saying as it relates to real estate: Location, Location, Location, Location is everything in retail, and the same applies to craft malls. Tourist locations are great because they usually get lots of traffic. Walking or browsing traffic can definitely help with sales. A mall heavily traveled is usually a successful mall.

Before you rent space in a mall, you might want to look around and ask a few questions. Find out how long current vendors have been with the mall. Have they had any theft problems, and if so, how was it handled? Do they have a fair amount of sales and how much traffic goes through the mall? To figure out what your rent should be, try to estimate what you think your average monthly sales would be. You should not be paying any more than 30% to 40% of what you sell. So if your monthly sales are $500 and you use 30% as your guide, you would multiply $500 x 30% to equal $150, indicating that your rent in the mall should be no more than $150 a month. Be sure to average out your monthly sales because in some months you will sell more than in others, such as before major holidays. Get your average sales figure by adding up all your sales for a year and dividing that figure by 12. Use this figure to determine just how well the mall is benefiting you. Make sure you count in any orders or home parties you booked as a result of the advertising you got through your mall space.

After you've decided to rent a space, make your display appealing by using some of the tips we talked about in setting up your craft show booth.

ᏋᏛᏋᏛᏋᏛᏋᏛᏋᏛ

Inspirational Quote: "Twenty years from now you will be more disappointed by the things you didn't do than by the things you did do." Anonymous.

CHAPTER 13

SELLING ONLINE/ YOUR OWN WEB SITE

This is a major topic, and one thing that I hear all the time is, "if I only had a Web site I could sell my jewelry." First we need to establish exactly what a Web site will and will not do for you. Having a Web site is a great tool to help you sell. I repeat; having a Web site is a great **"TOOL TO HELP YOU SELL."** A Web site is like opening a shop in the corner on a dark street without neon lights. Now, if you open that shop on a dark street with neon lights and you advertise that you are there and you've got something great to sell, you will stand a better chance at building up a clientele and they will come to buy from you. In short, the lesson here is that a Web site should be built and promoted as you go about the business of selling your product. It is not a fast way to make a buck or to get rich quick. Setting up and operating your online business will have financial and work requirements. It also requires regular maintenance and open communication between you and your customers. Having a successful Web site will require good marketing along with good customer service. It can also allow you to market your jewelry with international exposure, at very little expense. I say little expense because I'm comparing the costs involved in having retail space. With that said, you may ask, "What is the difference between an online business and a face-to-face in- person business?" The answer is-very little. The process is the same; the method you use to conduct business is the only difference. On the plus side, having a Web presence means you can operate your business 24 hours a day, 7 days a week with or without a "brick and mortar" location.

So if having a Web presence is something you think you would like to use to help you grow your business, start thinking up ways to promote your site. Having your business cards and any other promotional material with your

URL on it can definitely help you build your business, whether you sell at trunk shows, craft shows or through a rep. I promoted my business for years by passing out my cards with my Web address on them. Now that I am not doing shows, my Web site continues to thrive, literally on its own.

In conclusion, having a Web presence is an inexpensive form of continuous marketing and it can definitely help you build your business. Now, let's address some of the issues involved in setting up, maintaining and operating your own Web site.

I'm assuming you've already chosen your Web site name. Choosing the right name is extremely important. You should choose a name that is easy to remember or that is related to your jewelry in some way. After choosing your domain name, one of the first things you will need to do is register it. Your first question may be, what is a domain name? A domain name is your first impression to the outside world. Simply put, it's your address on the Internet, or your URL. It's where people will be able to find you. Your domain name will be made up of two parts, with "www" preceding your primary name. For example: www.yourname.com. The second part ".com" is the extension, which in this case stands for commercial. Besides .com, your extension could end in .net, .biz, .info or one of several others.

Acquiring your Web site domain name is easy, but first you will have to check to see if the name you want is already taken. You can do this by simply typing, "check domain name" in the browser on your computer. There are numerous sites that can check to see if your potential name is available. They can also register your URL. I prefer using "Yahoo" or "Go Daddy." Simply type in the name you want and you will know if it is available. If the name you want is taken, you will have to come up with an alternative name. The .com extensions are usually taken first but you will probably be able to get the name you want using .net, .biz or some other ending. One word of caution,

I don't recommend using any of the other endings because .com is the more common ending, so try to rework your name so that it ends in "dot com."

Over the last few years, purchasing or registering your Web site name/URL has become very competitive, so shop around on the Web to get the best price. Prices are usually quoted for one year, so each year you will have to renew your name. Don't worry, registering and renewing your site is very inexpensive.

Some Web hosts will register you and pay for your name, while others will register for you with you paying the InterNIC fees (see explanation of InterNIC below). One word of advice, register your name yourself so that you can be sure you are not only the registered owner, but that you are listed as the administrator and technical contact. Other important pieces of information to have when registering a Web host are its DNS IP address and the names of its primary and secondary nameservers. This can usually be found somewhere on their site. If you can't find it, e-mail the Webmaster and ask for it. If you don't have a Web host yet, all is not lost. Read on.

IMPORTANT TIPS TO REMEMBER WHEN CHOOSING YOUR NAME AND REGISTERING IT.

❑ Choose a domain name that reflects your business name or the topic your site will cover.

❑ Your name should be unique, concise and easy to remember.

❑ If your first choice isn't available, try rearranging the word order or add abbreviations etc. to come up with an alternative.

❑ The main part of your name can only contain letters a-z, digits 0-9, and a dash (-).

❑ If you use a dash, it can't be at the beginning or at the end of your name.

- Your name may not exceed 63 characters, excluding your .com, .biz etc.

- Underscore (_) and other special characters are not allowed.

- It usually takes 24 to 48 hours to activate a new domain. The "who is" search is the final search for your name. Wait at least 48 hours and check again.

- By typing in "register domain name" into your browser you will find numerous companies offering this service with prices varying widely. Remember that any company that sells domain names must be registered and accredited with Icann, which stands for Internet Corporation for Assigned Names and Numbers (refer to references in the back of this book for their Web site address).

- When registering your name, make sure your name is listed as the "administrative contact" with InterNIC. InterNIC stands for Internet Network Information Center. It is the governing body that is responsible for domain names. By listing your name as the contact you will be able to transfer your domain name to another Web Host/Internet Service Provider without any hassle, if you choose to. In short you will own your name. Make sure that your Web-site developer isn't listed as the administrative contact, or it may be difficult to switch to a new developer, if you need to. You will find more information about this in the next topic.

HOW TO CHOOSE A GOOD WEBHOST

This is one of the most important decisions you will have to make for your Web site. There are so many Web hosts or ISPs (Internet Service Providers) with a variety of services. Here's a quick rundown of the things you absolutely need to know before you sign up:

- ✓ Disk space – How much space will you have? For a small-size Web site, 10 to 20mb (megabits) should be sufficient; however, the more graphics you have, the more space you may need. You may want to ask if your mail files are counted in the total megabits of space offered. If so, they can take up space so you will probably need more. Remember, the more space you have, the more room you have in which to grow.

- ✓ How big is the pipeline? The pipeline is simply the speed at which your host is connected to the Internet. You will find most are connected by T1 and T3 lines. A T1 line can carry 1.5 megabits per second, while a T3 can carry 45 megabits per second, so go with as much as you can get. Go with T3 or higher.

- ✓ How many visitors or how much Bandwidth will you have? Bandwidth determines the amount of data transfer allowed each month. Let's say you will get lots of traffic on your Web site during the holiday season and you have restrictions on how many hits or visitors you can have. If you go over your limit you can be charged extra for each hit. Bandwidth of 1GB can support at least 3,000 visitors, so read the fine print.

- ✓ Make sure your Web host/ISP provider offers virtual hosting/domain. This is extremely important because if you change providers you won't have to change your name. Having virtual hosting or a virtual domain will allow you to have your own domain name, such as www.pudgybeads.com rather than use your hosts name with a subdirectory to your site, such as www.yahoo.com/pudgybeads/.

- ✓ With a virtual domain you should ask how many e-mail addresses are allowed. This is called pop3. Pop3 simply allows

139

you to have an e-mail address with your own domain name. Most Host/ISP's will allow you to set up multiple "aliases" such as sales@pudgybeads.com or info@pudgybeads.com. This may be important to you as you grow.

✓ How much support will you have? Good technical support is a must. You will need to know how many hours a day live support is available. I would never go with a Web host/ISP provider who didn't offer live support. E-mail only support just doesn't work; trying to communicate this way is both frustrating and ineffective. Even if you have to pay a little more to have live support, do it … it will be money well spent.

Your Web host/ISP provider should guarantee 99% uptime for your Web site, (uptime is simply the amount of time your site is available to be seen). Ask them, if it's not prominently displayed on their Web site. Be sure to ask for referrals so that if you feel it's necessary, you can contact current customers about their level of service.

FREE OR PAY WEBHOST?

Should you pay for your Web host or choose a free one? The decision is up to you. There are both positives and negatives. One major plus in using a paid host is that you will have full control over the content on your Web site. In my opinion your site will have a more professional image without advertisements, banners and pop-ups floating across your pages. If you choose a free host, usually you will have limited or no technical support, along with the possibility of unreliable servers and software. Along with limited Web space, your web address will have the Internet provider's name before yours, so instead of www.yourname.com, your Web address might look like this: www.inernetprovidersname/yourname.com. Now that you know some of the pluses and minuses, choose whatever you feel comfortable with or can afford. There are plenty of free Web hosting services out there, so the choice is yours.

CREATING YOUR WEB SITE

When it comes to creating your Web site, you will have lots of decisions to make, such as what kind of overall image you want to convey? What kind of software you will use? What kind of style you want? How do you want your site to be structured? What color do you want your pages to be? How will you take your pictures? Will you use a scanner or a digital camera? All the questions you may have can leave you feeling overwhelmed, so let's tackle these questions one by one.

❑ First things first. Surf the Net and check out Web sites that appeal to you, then bookmark them. Identify why you like them. Is it the style? Is it because it's easy to move around (navigate) in? Try to get a feel for what type of image you want your site to convey. All these things will come in handy as you prepare to construct your Web site.

❑ Before you start building your actual site, use a pen and paper to construct all of your pages. Start with a circle in the middle of the page - this circle is your homepage. From the homepage circle, draw branch pages. These branch pages will contain the pages that will connect to, and be listed, on your homepage. If you need any related branches to extend from any of the secondary branches, just connect them. Remember, your Web site should be logical and should flow smoothly. This drawing is the beginning of your navigation structure. Navigation structure simply refers to the order in which you want your pages to connect. The technical name for these connections is hyperlinks. Carefully planning the structure of your Web site will make it easy for visitors to find their way around. Have you ever visited a site and found it difficult and confusing to find what you wanted? This is the result of poor navigation planning. Take your time and think about how you want to connect your pages.

❑ In your pre-site planning be sure to decide what background color, background theme, font color, font size, and font type you want. If you use wallpaper, make sure you choose one that is subtle; after all you want to sell your product, not the wallpaper. Make sure you have plenty of contrast between your text and page color. I've been on sites where the text was barely readable. When designing your site keep in mind that you want your jewelry to stand out on the page, so keep it simple.

❑ Choosing software to construct your Web page is something that will require research on your part. A good place to start is by asking friends or business associates what software they used for their Web site. Find out the pros and cons. Utilize the Internet by doing an online search by simply typing "Web page software" into your browser. I used Front Page for my site. Front Page is uncomplicated and easy to use. If you can use Microsoft Word, Front Page is just as easy. Its language consists of WYSIWYG (what you see is what you get). Be sure to check out some of the Shareware sites, these Web sites allow you to use software for 30 days and buy it if you like it. I think it's a great way to try it out before you make the commitment.

❑ If you feel confused and inadequate when it comes to using software and feel that even the WYSIWYG software can throw you into a learning curve, some Web site providers/hosts offer Web site building templates. Most of these templates have "wizards" that even the most computer challenged person can follow because everything's been thought out for you. All you have to do is plug in your information and upload your pictures. A great site to check out is "Shopping Cart Plus and Homestead." Both are easy and uncomplicated to use.

❑ Make sure the photos of your jewelry are as clear, bright, and sharp as possible. It doesn't matter if you use a scanner or a digital camera. Save your pictures as a JPEG, or GIF file. When deciding between GIF and JPEG the most important things to remember is that GIF photos work best on solid colors and sharp-edged transitions from one color to another and GIF is limited in the total number of colors to 256 or less. JPEG works best on continuous gradations of many colors or grey tones, such as color or black and white photographs. JPEG files do not handle sharp edges as well as GIF, blurring them a little. When in doubt, try both ways and see which looks better. For more in-depth information on photos for your Web site, visit some of the links on our resource pages.

❑ Use good editing software to edit your photos. Simple, low-cost software like Adobe Photoshop Elements and Paint Shop Pro will do all the editing, resizing, trimming, brightening, contrasting and enhancing you will need. Also try Irfanview and Picasa for free editing software (see our resource pages for URLs).

❑ If you are using a scanner, you can use lace, fabric, embossed paper or whatever you want to produce an uncluttered background. Tape the paper or fabric to a large baking pan and place this over your scanner when you scan. Keep in mind that a scanner is like a mirror so using the baking pan to cover your items will give you a great background. The baking pan will also keep your arranged items from moving while on the scanner because of the space on the inside of the pan. Another hint for getting great pictures is to make sure the scanner glass and your jewelry are free of any dust or debris. You can use a little alcohol on a tissue to keep your scanner bed clean.

- Is your site graphic heavy? The more pictures you have, the slower your page will load. Use thumbnails. Thumbnails are tiny images that are linked to a larger image. When you click on your thumbnail you will be directed to a screen that will display a full-size image. Haven't you been on sites where the photos are too tiny to see? I have, and what a waste. Remember, your pictures are the only things that connect you to your buyer, so having a photo large enough to be seen is very important.

- Banners ... oh how I hate them. If you've visited any Web sites, you've seen them. Usually they are brightly colored or animated, or both. If you choose to use a free Web host (ISP) provider, more than likely they will imbed these distracting, annoying things as ads, which is why you get hosting services without paying. You've heard it before, "there are no free rides."

- Animations, I wouldn't, but if you must have them, then by all means use no more than one on a page. Animations are those little moving, twirling, bouncing cute pictures you see on some Web sites. I personally think they are distracting, and they will make your page load slower; but if you insist, use a GIF animation, they are much easier to use and see.

- Music, is nice, but not on my Web page. Aah, but again, if you insist, please place a volume control on your page. This way the person viewing your site can easily control the volume. Music also increases your page loading time ... so think about it.

❑ Creating your homepage – Since this page is the most important page, what's included and not included on this page can make or break a visitor's decision to explore a Web site. This is where making every word count will definitely help your site; please don't use fluffy filler words. Haven't you ever bought a magazine while standing in line at the supermarket because of the teasers on the cover? Use this same approach for your Web site and you will capture and keep your audience. Make your descriptions interesting and informative. Make sure your homepage is attractive, and as previously discussed, clear and simple to move around in. Make sure the word/text content on this page includes a description of what you are about, along with key words that pertain to what you do. Remember, your one-or two-sentence description shows up in the search engine results, so choose them carefully. Do some research to find words or phrases that are relevant to the content on your site. Include these words or phrases in your title, description and in your web site copy. For instance, if your jewelry is "vintage jewelry" or "wire jewelry" use these as your key words. These key words or phrases are called "meta tags". Meta tags supply information about the content on your Web page. They are not visible when people view your page. They can only be viewed in HTML. HTML is the language that all Web pages are constructed in. Even if you use a program like FrontPage to construct your Web site, HTML is the language that you can't see, however it is the code language that is read by the Internet.

❑ Before you launch your site, make sure all of your links work and test them often to avoid dead or broken links.

WHAT YOU CAN DO TO OPTIMIZE YOUR WEB SITE

First let's define exactly what optimizing your web site is. Most people use search-engines to locate Web sites that offer what they are looking for by typing key words into the browser. Being listed within the first 100 search results is what you should strive for. Having your site listed in the first few pages can without a doubt bring you potential customers. Using search-engines to optimize your site is one way to achieve this. Search-engine optimizing, placement, positioning or ranking are all terms used to describe where your Web site comes up in a given search. Search-engine submission refers to the act of getting your Web site listed with search-engines. Getting listed with the search-engines doesn't mean you will come up in the first few pages; it simply means that the search-engines know your site exists. Think of it as purchasing a ticket to a contest, having the ticket doesn't mean you will win, but you must have the ticket to have a chance at winning.

Space doesn't permit me to go into great detail about optimizing your Web site, so go online and type "Optimizing Web site" into your browser for detailed information. Remember, optimizing or bringing traffic to your site does not necessarily mean you will get sales, since it represents only one way to get your site noticed.

Here are some suggestions on optimizing and getting your site noticed.

1) **First and most important** is designing the pages on your site to be as search-engine friendly as possible. Using the right keywords will help bring traffic to your site. Key words or phrases are the words people enter when they search for information online. Whatever your key words are, be sure to include them on each of your Web site pages, sprinkling them liberally throughout the pages without overdoing it. If you are unsure about what your key words should be, try researching what they should be rather than

146

guessing at it. The search-engine Web site "What People Search For" and "Searchenginewatch" is listed on our resource pages to assist you if you need help.

2) **Having a title** that is precise and will relay to visitors what they will find on your site is very important. Use short, specific attention-grabbing titles. If you can, include your key word/phrase in your title or come as close to it as possible.

3) **Promote your site** by whatever method you've chosen to sell your product. Make sure all promotional material has your Web site address on it. I love using color postcards (see resource page for postcard printers) with several pictures of my product and all contact information, including my Web address. Passing these out freely will do more to promote your site than any Web page optimizing you can do. Of course, using personal promotions along with whatever optimizing you do can only help in making your site a success.

4) **To achieve a higher ranking,** which translates into more traffic on your site, you will need to submit your site to major search engines. For a hefty fee, there are companies that will swear that they hold the key to increasing traffic on your site. Before you pay for a service like that, submit your own site. In the first few months of having my Web site I would resubmit my site every two or three weeks. I even adjusted my Meta tags and Web site copy a couple of times until I got the ranking I wanted. Now my Web site comes up on the first few pages of most major search-engines. Trying to get links to your site by linking to already established sites will definitely help you get listed. So put your mind to work and see how your site can tie into more established ones.

5) **Submit to Open Directories** - Open directories are volunteer-built guides to the Web, in short they are powered by human editors who compile all the listings in the directory. Many people see these listings and the crawler/computer-generated search-engines are more likely to find your site and add it to their listings for free. It is provided as an option at many major search engines. Being listed with the open directory is essential to any site owner. Make sure you take some time to learn more about the open directories before submitting your site, this way you can maximize the amount of traffic you may receive, which is your goal. Previously we talked about the description of your Web site; this is where you would use your well-prepared description along with your two or three key words and phrases. When submitting to an open directory or any search-engine, make sure you choose the right category to submit to and take time to find out exactly how they want their descriptions and titles written.

"TIP" Just submitting your Web site to the major search-engines is not enough to get a good ranking. Make sure your Web site is optimized before you do your submissions.

THE FOLLOWING FREE AND PAID SUBMISSIONS CAN HELP YOU GET STARTED:

FREE SUBMISSION URLs TO LIST YOUR SITE:

- http://www.alltheweb.com/add_url.php - submit your homepage and a couple of inside pages. This one takes about six weeks before your pages appear.

- http://www.google.com/addurl.html - Goggle is a top choice for searchers. If you manage to get listed here your results will also appear

148

in Yahoo and AOL. Submit your homepage and a couple of other pages; it will take about a month before your pages appear.

- http://www.altavista.com/addurl/new - You can add up to five URLs to be considered in 4-6 weeks. Again, submit your homepage and one or two other pages.

- http://www.inktomi.com/products/web_search/submit.html - Submit homepage and two or three other pages.

- http://ask.ineedhits.com - If you manage to get listed here you will also be connected with Ask.com. Their partners include Excite, MySearch.com, and Mamma.com.

PAID SUBMISSION URLs TO LIST YOUR SITE:

- https://www.infospider.com/av/app/signup - Alta Vista

Submit your homepage. Your pages will be listed within two weeks and revisited regularly at a reasonable price. They offer a six-month subscription. If you don't renew, your pages will definitely be dropped.

- http://insite.lycos.com/inclusion/searchenginesubmit.asp?- Lycos

I think this one is a great deal and well worth the money. It takes 72 hours to get listed. Your pages will be visited every two days for one year. This is a good option if you want a new site to get listed fast.

- http://ask.ineedhits.com - Ask Jeeves

Submit your homepage and your site will be listed within one week. It's definite that your pages will be dropped if you don't renew.

- Inktomi's search engine has an extensive network of Web search partners, including MSN, About, Hotbot and Overture. It refreshes your site every 48 hours. Submit your homepage and your site will be listed in 2 days and will be regularly revisited up to one year. Your pages may be dropped if you don't renew your subscription.

HOW TO INCREASE YOUR RANKING WITH LINKING

Getting search-engines to list your Web site on the first few pages of a search is what you are after. Linking your site to other Web sites is just as important as the content and keywords on your homepage. The more popular your Web site is, the better the search engines rank it. In fact, linking is one of the best ways for Goggle and other sought-after search-engines to find you. These search-engines are equipped with mechanisms that jump from page to page on the Web by hyperlinks, so the more sites that link to you, the more likely you will be found. Linking to just any site will not get you what you want. Search-engines look very carefully at who is linking to you, and what they are saying about you. Getting links from bead societies, show listings or any organization you've sold or donated to will definitely help. Getting links to random unrelated sites will not help you; links like these are considered low quality.

Free for all sites called "Link Farms," fall into the poor link category. Getting linked to this kind of low-quality link will not help you at all. Other sites you should not be associated with are sites that have been penalized by search-engines for spamming. It won't be held against you if they link to you, but it will if you link back to them because you are held responsible for the links you place on your site.

The search-engines will consider things like key phrases that are used in the link space on your site, along with information on related organizations. If you specialize in vintage jewelry, have a page with information on vintage jewelry along with some books on the subject. Offer to link with distributors of the books you recommend. Offer a link to the stores you sell to. You shouldn't have any trouble finding jewelry or fashion-related sites. If you use crystal in your jewelry, try linking to crystal handbags, crystal hair ornaments or any non-competing items that use crystals. If you are participating in a craft fair or bazaar, offer a link to their site along with a few other artists that are selling at the event. You get the idea, finding and coordinating sites that would benefit from your site's link can help you too. Going about this in a meticulous, organized manner can benefit you tremendously.

HOW TO SOLICIT LINKS

To solicit sites you will have to spend time sending out personalized e-mails to the sites you want to link too. Point out the benefits of them linking to your site. If you are lucky, maybe one in three e-mails will get a response. Some sites don't update often. If a site hasn't been updated in years, skip it. Even though it may seem tempting, don't send out mass e-mails. Keep a word file on who you have contacted and a copy of what you wrote. You have to make it seem like they are the only person you are contacting, so that if you have to communicate with them, you will be able to do so without embarrassment. Remember, if the site you are contacting thinks that you are doing mass e-mails you will definitely not get their link.

Remember links are more valuable to search-engines if your name or URL appears in a sentence or paragraph rather than just in a listing. Search-engines assume your site is worthy of getting noticed if you are in the content of a page. However, don't turn down being listed in a group of links related to what you sell, because people who visit those sites while surfing may just click on your site link and you may get some unsuspected traffic.

Having a one-way or "non-reciprocal" link is very valuable to search engines and will make your site rate highly. Search-engines regard this type of link highly because it shows that someone wanted to send people who visited their site to yours without expecting anything in return. Keep in mind that not all reciprocal links are bad, if you choose some that you think will benefit you. Adding your link to a site that you might benefit from and e-mailing the

Webmaster that you have added their link to your site is something you should try. Ask them if they will add you as a link. Allow a month or so and if you don't hear anything and your site is not linked to theirs, take their site off yours and e-mail someone else for links. Even after you are linked, check back occasionally to make sure you are still linked. Again, make sure you keep your word file updated.

While in the process of targeting your list of links, you can try out some of the free link exchange sites, like "linkslister" and "Value Exchange." These sites are designed to make link-swapping easy. Remember your key words; this is where, if you have carefully chosen them, they will reward you with great link matches.

OTHER WAYS TO PROMOTE YOUR SITE

1. There are guides on the Internet that can help you promote your Web site and provide you with interesting information. Most of these sites will let you acquire linking, write jewelry-related articles or provide you with a permanent link. Send the individual who is responsible for the section you are interested in information about your site with an invitation to visit. If your site impresses the guide, you may stand a chance of being mentioned on their Web site pages with a permanent link. Some of these guides also issue awards to sites that are considered "best of the web." Maybe your site will be chosen … it's worth a shot. "Jewelry-Paideia" is my favorite because its devoted strictly to jewelry, See our resource page for a listing of guide sites.

2. Become involved in chat rooms, bulletin boards, discussion lists or any other networking group. Any crafter's/artisan's guild, bead society or women business-owner's group is ideal, too. Joining these types of groups can help you in lots of ways, including

finding potential customers, suppliers, referrals, marketing tips and general business information. Besides joining groups online, if there are local groups in your area, it would definitely benefit you to become involved. Attending a meeting every other month or so can benefit you by presenting you with networking/business card-exchange opportunities.

Inspirational Quote: "Courage is going from failure to failure without losing enthusiasm," Winston Churchill.

CHAPTER 14

SELLING ONLINE WITHOUT A WEB SITE

Selling online using auctions or co-op sites can be a great way to sell. Particularly if you want to use this way of selling along with participating in a few craft shows or other methods of selling. Ebay is the most well known auction-selling site. If you decide to sell on Ebay, don't kid yourself; you will have plenty of competition. We've all heard about numerous success stories on Ebay and most are probably true, especially the earlier stories when Ebay did not have the large volume of people who sell now. To succeed in this vast pool of sellers you will have to be unique or stand out in some way. If selling on Ebay is the way you want to sell, you should start first by doing the same thing you would do with any other way of selling-analyze your competition. Go online and type in your browser www.ebay.com. Use this time to explore the site and browse through your potential competitors, make notes on their price points, styles and materials used. Bookmark a few selected competitors and track their sales progress. You might also like to take Ebay's guided tour and visit their discussion boards. Ebay has a learning center where you can take a free audio tour and courses online. You can also sign up at Ebay University; their courses will guide you through all the fine points of getting started with them. At the university you also can sign up for selling basics, which will guide you through the entire selling process. Ebay University also offers day-long teaching seminars in various areas throughout the country. You can find out specific times and dates by visiting their Web site.

At Ebay.com/community, you can access chat groups and discussion boards. Speaking of community, there is an online group of women who use

Ebay to sell full time. They are called "powerchicks." These empowered women have forged a living by using this venue as their only way to sell.

Before you can start selling on Ebay, you will need to set up a Seller's Account, this is a simple process. It is very similar to the registration process only it includes providing Ebay with information to verify your identity and your preferred method of paying seller fees.

On Ebay you can sell using auction-style listings, sell at a fixed price, or open an Ebay Store. An Ebay Store provides a consistent location for your listings and merchandise and is an excellent place to sell add-on merchandise. It's also an inexpensive and simple way to establish an e-commerce presence.

You can also set up an "About Me" page. This is a free Ebay feature that allows you to promote your business.

Selling is straightforward on Ebay, if you post your listings through an auction-style post or a "buy it now" post. Your auctions can be listed for one to 10 days; the average is seven. The "buy it now" listing allows sellers to sell the product at a set price.

Tips for listing your auctions

· Make sure your pictures are sharp and clear. Follow our suggestions in a previous chapter on taking good photos.

· Ebay does not allow you to store your pictures on their servers. For space to store your pictures, check with your Internet service provider. Most providers provide a limited amount of free storage space. You can upload your pictures to the Internet by using an FTP program. FTP stands for file transfer protocol. It is used to connect two computers over the Internet so that the user of one computer can transfer files (your JPEG pictures) and perform file commands on the other computer. Although this may sound complicated, it's really a very simple procedure.

Major Tip: *Remember, buyers cannot physically touch or see your items, so clear, sharp pictures and detailed accurate listings are the only things they have when deciding whether or not to make the purchase.*

- Take some time to decide on your title. Your title is really the most important part of your auction; after all, it is this feature that attracts buyers to view your description. Your title is what the buyer sees first; make sure you stick to key words, such as materials or techniques used. Choose words that buyers would search for when looking for your item. Be sure to include any special details about the jewelry you are selling.

- The description of the jewelry you are selling is extremely important. Include as much accurate information as possible, such as color and texture, size or dimensions, beads used, etc. Clearly state the condition of the item and make sure you accurately describe any defects.

- Be prepared to offer good customer service. Include your accepted methods of payment, shipping cost, and return policy. This is important because Ebay users can post feedback about your quality of service and care. These comments will be tallied to offer your overall Ebay rating. Positive comments on these feedback ratings can increase your score and negative comments can make your score go down. Potential buyers view these ratings, so they are very important.

Besides Ebay, there are many other successful commercial sites where you can sell your jewelry. I actually prefer these smaller sites because of their size and their specialties. Online craft-marketing co-ops are like miniature craft shows. You will find direct links to several online craft-marketing sites on our resource pages.

Wholesale Crafts is one of the larger selling sites where crafters pay an advertising fee to be listed in a Buyers Guide. The buyers guide is then distributed free to retailers. This is a way of bringing crafters and retailers together at reasonable expense.

Another great site is ECrafters. ECrafters gives you a forum to sell your craft items free. They offer lots of advantages to make your e-commerce experience easier. They also provide a craft-fair event listing.

Ruby Lane is another site devoted to selling; they provide you with an easy to use template to build your own storefront of up to 20 items. You are also included in their store directory. Another plus is that your site will be submitted monthly to the search engines.

My favorite site for selling without a Web site is Etsy. I like this site because it is not an auction site but it gives you an online presence and a chance for your handmade items to be placed among other crafters' items. Etsy gives every seller his own shop, free of charge along with a Web site address. You can even customize your shop. Every item you list for sale will automatically show up in your shop. They will also be placed in the category you listed them in. On Etsy, your items are listed for six months, with only a small fee for each listing. One of the best features of Etsy is that it submits your Web site to Goggle's search engine. Everything about setting up your site and selling on Etsy is easy, from the registration process to setting up your shop.

ഏ✧ഏ✧ഏ✧ഏ✧ഏ✧

Inspirational quote: "Success is when you work hard at something and you can still smile," Anonymous.

THE END

I am having a wild and wonderful ride in my jewelry career as I continue to provide accessories to a limited number of premier house accounts. This business has enabled me to realize my strengths as well as my weaknesses. It has given me the thrill of seeing my business thrive and grow. It has allowed me to dream and have options in my life. It has allowed me to travel throughout the United States doing shows and visit other countries, including the Czech Republic, Germany, France and London, to name a few. It has enabled me to open a successful retail store, but what this business has truly given me is a network of wonderful people throughout the world who have become dear friends and colleagues. Through it all, I've been able to earn a great living, it has empowered me, and it has made me strive to be the best at whatever I do. And it can do the same for you.

Whether you decide to sell online or off, in boutiques or at craft fairs, if you have decided that you are committed to making your business work for you, then "make it happen." Remember, no matter which way you decide to sell, be consistent … set up a realistic plan and stick to it. It is my hope that you have gained valuable information from reading my book and that it will help guide you through whatever path you choose.

We live in a constantly changing world, and there are always new directions to take; so stay open and inquisitive. Be imaginative, think outside the box and remember, with determination and hard work you truly can make your jewelry line a success. Good luck!

ഗ്രൂഗ്രൂഗ്രൂഗ്രൂഗ്രൂ

Inspirational quote: "If you think you can, dream you can, apply all that you can, you will become all that you can" Susie Edwards.

RESOURCE PAGES

INFORMATION ABOUT CRAFT/PROFESSIONAL SHOWS

http://festivalnet.com

http://www.craftlister.com/events

http://www.craftmall.com/

http://www.artsandcraftshows.com

http://www.craftsfaironline.com

http://www.craftmasternews.com

http://www.tradeshowbiz.com - a complete listing of professional tradeshows throughout the country, including jewelry and accessories.

RESOURCES FOR FINDING PROFESSIONAL REPS

(Hint, when looking on these Web sites look for "Apparel and Accessories market weeks")

LOS ANGELES, CA: http:// www.californiamarketcenter.com

SAN FRANCISCO, CA: http://www.gcjm.com/

MARKET WEEK SAN FRANCISCO: http://www.fashionsanfrancisco.com

DALLAS, TEXAS: http://www.dallasmarketcenter.com

ATLANTA, GEORGIA: http://www.americasmart.com

CHICAGO, ILLINOIS: http://www.merchandisemart.com/apparelcenter

MIAMI, FLORIDA: http://www.miamimart.net/

DENVER, CO: http://www.denvermart.com/martset.html

PROFESSIONAL SHOWS (primarily for production lines):

SHOW	LOCATION	WEB SITE
ACCESSORIESTHESHOW	JACOB JAVITS CENTER, NEW YORK, N.Y.	WWW.ACCESSORIESTHESHOW.COM
Accessories the show is the longest running accessory trade event in the United States. This edited show covers every category of accessories. Sponsored by Accessories Magazine.		
ACCESSORIE CIRCUIT	THE PIER NEW YORK, N.Y.	WWW.ENKSHOWS.COM
Accessorie Circuit is a juried accessories and footwear show for Women. High-end costume-jewelry to fine jewelry.		
MAGIC THE SHOW	LAS VEGAS CONVENTION CENTER	WWW.SHOW.MAGICONLINE
This show is the largest most comprehensive women's apparel and accessory trade event in the United States. It's put on in conjunction with Women's Wear Daily. It serves the following markets: contemporary, junior apparel and accessories.		
ASD/AMD JEWELRY SHOW	MIRAGE HOTEL, LAS VEGAS, NEVADA	WWW.MERCHANDISEGROUP.COM
The accessories show is held in conjunction with three other shows, there are hundreds of fine and fashion jewelry exhibitors combined with cross-market purchasing opportunities		

HOW TO GET YOUR ONE OF A KIND ITEMS INTO A GALLERY:

http://www.craftsreport.com

160

ORGANIZATIONS YOU MAY NEED

Chamber of Commerce - Contact them at www.chamberofcommerce.com
Small Business Administration - Contact them at http://www.sba.gov/
SCORE – Contact them at www.score.com

MAGAZINES & NEWSPAPERS

Accessories magazine - http://www.accessoriesmagazine.com/jewelry.shtml
Accessories magazine is the leading publication in the world of accessories.
This magazine is a good option for designers. It's loaded with timely fashion
trends, retail profiles and relevant information for accessory designers. Twice a
year they publish "Directions" which is an accessory trend-forecasting
magazine, a tremendous asset to designers, without the cost of paying for a
trend service.

California Apparel News - http://www.apparelnews.net
California Apparel News Group is a weekly newspaper to keep you up-to-date
on women's, men's and children's apparel information.

Art Jewelry Magazine - http://www.artjewelrymag.com
This magazine is published six times a year and features inspirational artists to
help advance your design skill level.

Jewelry Crafts - http://www.jewelrycraftsmag.com/ - This magazine is project
oriented with how-to instructions. It covers mostly beginners and intermediate
projects

Women's Wear Daily (WWD) - http://www.wwd.com/ - This newspaper,
often called "the fashion bible," focuses on the fashion, beauty, and retail
industries.

Wire Artist Jewelers - http://www.wag.on.ca/index.html - This magazine is
dedicated to wire artist. It has great projects and photos.

WEB SITE RESOURCES

LINK EXCHANGES

http://www.linkslister.com/ - free link exchange
http://www.telalinks.com/ - free link exchange
http://value-exchange.sitesell.com/ - free link exchange
http://linkpopularity.com - This site will allow you to input your Web site
and see how many links you have to your site.

http://searchenginewatch.com This site is helpful for promoting your Web site.

SOFTWARE, INTERNET PROVIDERS AND SUCH

http://www.thefreecountry.com - This Web site offers the best-of-the-best of free programming resources, including software, tutorials, and almost anything you need to know about creating, keeping and using a Web site.

http://www.dmoz.org - This is the Web site of the Open Directory Project, which is the largest, most comprehensive human-edited directory of the Web. It is constructed and maintained by a vast, global community of volunteer editors.

http://www.searchenginewatch.com - what people search for – most popular key words.

http://www.thelist.com - The List™is intended as a resource for people looking for an Internet service provider. This international listing will allow you to search by area code or by country code.

http://www.webstudio.com - Easy Web-building software, with a 30-day free trial.

http://www.smartftp.com - This site is a FTP (file transfer protocol) site, which allows you to transfer files between your local computer and a server on the Internet.

http://www.coffeecup.com - This site offers lots of different software, including excellent FTP software for you to download.

http://www.coreftp.com - This site offers free FTP software…a steal!

http://www.softpedia.com - Another free FTP site!
http://www.lview.com - Photo editing software
http://www.corel.com - Photo editing software
http://www.irfanview.com/ - Free photo editing software
http://picasa.google.com/ - Free photo editing software
http://www.download.com/Pixia - This free photo editing software will not only edit your pictures, but will watermark them, too.

Domain name registrars

(There are numerous registrars. Listed below are just a few.)

http://smallbusiness.yahoo.com/domains - well known in the domain registration world, they even give you a starter page for your Web site.

http://www.godaddy.com - the world's largest registrar. They offer a free starter Web page, a free parked page or a free "for sale" page.

1&1 Internet Inc - a free e-mail account with up to 200 e-mail aliases and a starter Web site builder.

CREDIT CARD PROCESSING

https://www.2checkout.com/

http://www.merchantwarehouse.com/

http://www.creditcardequip.com/merchantaccounts.cfm

http://www.merchantseek.com/buyersguide/chap3/sec9.htm
http://www.2checkout.com/home.html
http://www.ccnow.com/

WEB SITES WITH INFO RELATED TO CHARITABLE CAUSES

http://en.wikipedia.org/wiki/List_of_awareness_ribbons - This site will give you a complete listing of awareness ribbons

http://www.raisingcancerawareness.com - This site will give you all the cancer awareness colors.

http://www.makingmemories.org - This organizations focus is to advance the awareness of breast cancer and to educate the public about the vast resources and support available to breast cancer patients and their families."

www.beadingforacure.org - Layne's Legacy is an annual beading challenge dedicated to raising money for the National Colorectal Cancer Research Association.

http://www.jewelrycampaign.net/eng/index.htm - Campaigns that addresses violations of workers' rights in the garment and jewelry industry.

ONLINE CRAFT MARKETING SITES

Wholesalecrafts - http://www.wholesalecrafts.com

ECrafters - http://www.ecrafter.com

Etsy - http://www.etsy.com

Ruby lane - www.rubylane.com

Wire Jewelry Artist - www.jewelryartistdirect.com

Handcrafted Artist site - http://www.electroniccottage.com

FORUMS & GUIDES

http://www.about.com
http://www.suite101.com/
http://www.jewelry-paideia.com/
http://forums.ebay.com
http://www.ganoksin.com

http://forums.delphiforums
http://www.doxallo.com/forum/
http://jewelrymaking.bellaonline.com
http://www.beadinghelpweb.com/
http://urbanfool.us/forum/
http://www.beadandbutton.com/bnb/community/forum/
http://groups.msn.com/onebeadatatime
http://www.beadstylemag.com/bds/community/forum
http://groups.yahoo.com/group/Wire_Wrap_Jewelry/
http://wirejewelrydesignandtechniquesforum
http://www.warmglass.com
http://www.jewelryandbeading.com
http://www.isgb.org/forum - International society of glass bead makers
http://www.wirejewelryartists.org/index.html

PERSONALIZED STAMPS/TAGS FOR YOUR JEWELRY

http://www.infinitystamps.com/index.html.

http://www.microstampusa.com

http://www.harpermfg.com/hm_jewelrystamps.html

SITES YOU MAY WANT TO VISIT

Biz women – http://www.bizjournals.com/bizwomen. This great online resource is for women in business, it facilitates networking, offers business advice. It's a great marketplace for women owned and operated businesses.

American Craft Council - http://www.americancraft.com/ a great resource site with a variety of information related to the arts.

Cloud Dome - http://www.clouddomeproductions.com - visit this site for items you may need to make your digital photos better.

http://www.webpagesthatsuck.com - This funny and informative site really does analyze web sites that in its opinion suck.

FASHION/ACCESSORY FORECASTERS

http://www.trendstop.com/ - Trendstop provides fashion forecasts and global trend information. It shows you how to translate trends into successful products in order to outsmart your competition. You can even download editable trend silhouettes for Illustrator and other design programs.

http://www.style.com - Too good to be free! This online home of Vogue & W features complete fashion-show coverage (the videos and photos are online right after the shows), the lowdown on celebrity style, trend reports, expert advice and breaking fashion news.

http://www.pantone.com - Nice presentation and easy navigation. Pantone provides color systems and technology across a variety of industries. They have products such as "Color Matching System," a book of standardized color in fan format. It is the reference for selecting, specifying, matching and controlling colors.

http://www.accessoriestheshow.com/trends – This site provides information about upcoming trends in jewelry

JEWELRY AND MARK-UP CALCULATORS

http://www.steinermarketing.com/calc_markup_pricing.htm
http://www.csgnetwork.com/retailsalescalc.html - retail sales calculator
http://www.pasternakfindings.com/calculator – jewelry markup calculator

SITES TO HELP YOU MAKE GOOD PICTURES:

http://store.tabletopstudio-store.com/index.html
http://www.connectedphotographer.com/issuesprint/issue200406/00001334.ht
ml
http://www.deadzoom.com/member/nktower/tutorials/Photographing_Small_O
bjects.html

POSTCARD PRINTER

Modern postcard…www.modernpostcard.com

BUSINESS NUMBERS & CONTACTS

Dunn & Bradstreet - (800) 333-0505.

Icann - Internet Corporation for Assigned Names and Numbers. Any company that sells domain names must be registered with this organization. Reach them at http://www.icann.org).

Internic – The governing body responsible for all domain names. Reach them at www.internic.com).

ক্ষসক্ষসক্ষসক্ষসক্ষস

The following pages contain completed sample forms.

To download copies of these forms and to access more

resource links, please visit www.pudgypublishing .com

ক্ষসক্ষসক্ষসক্ষসক্ষস

SAMPLE CATALOG AND SOURCE SHEET

Cataloging your line

1. Give all your jewelry styles a number starting at whatever number you wish. You can also give your accessories a name.

2. To catalog all your items, photocopy or scan your items. After your pieces are duplicated, place one photo per sheet and list all relevant information about the piece (see example). Be sure to include what suppliers your parts came from, along with their cost. List final prices, colors used and any relevant information about that style.

3. You may want to do two catalog books at the same time, one book containing all information such as sources and item numbers "for your eyes only" and the other book having pictures and style numbers only, with no sources or suppliers for customers or employees.

```
┌─────────────────────────────────┐
│                                 │
│        Photo or scan of item    │
│                                 │
│                                 │
│                                 │
└─────────────────────────────────┘
```

1 Onyx cabochon that measures @ 25x18 mm
Gold -filled filigree setting @ 25x18 mm
1 gold-filled Figaro chain measuring @ 18 inch
1 dozen of crème pearl Swarovski teardrops @ 7x8 mm

Onyx cabochon 25x18, purchased from Joe's bead shop, cost $2.00 each or in volume $18.00 for 10 pieces. Order number 1506. Telephone (222) 555-0000.

Gold-filled filigree setting, 25x18, purchased from the bead shop, (213) 555-0000, order number 661. Cost $3.00 each or in volume 10 pieces for $20.00.

Gold-filled figaro chain measuring 18 inches. Purchased from the bead shop (213) 555-0000. Order number 1212. Cost $5.00 per foot. The cost for this necklace is $7.50.

Crème Swarovski pearl teardrops, 7x8, purchased from bead world, (213) 555-0000
Order number 1886. Cost .50 (cents) each or $4.00 for 10 pieces.

PINK POLKA DOT JEWELRY
111 APRIL AVE., STE 124
LOS ANGELES, CA 90807
562-212-000
polkadotjew@heyyou.com
www.pinkpolkajew.com

CONSIGNMENT AGREEMENT WITH

Park Ave Boutique (name of store/gallery)
1150 2nd St (address)
Long Beach, Ca 90808 (City, St, zip)
562-222-0000 (telephone)
www.parkaveboutique.com (website)

BETWEEN: Pink Polka Dot Beads/Susie Edwards
(jewelry artist co name & personal name)
Herein referred to as "Artist"

111 April Ave., Suite 123, Los Angeles, CA 90807

(Your address)

562-444-0000 (your telephone no.)
pink polkadot@heyyou.com (your e-mail address)
www.pinkpolkadotjew.com (your Web site address)
AND:
Park Ave. Boutique (name of shop/boutique)
Herein referred to as "Shop"

RECITALS

The above-mentioned shop is in the business of retailing finished costume jewelry/beaded items.
The above-mentioned Artist has created, and owns items described on consignment product sheet.
THEREFORE, in consideration of mutual covenants and promises in this agreement

CONVENANTS/PROMISES OF SHOP

"Shop" promises, accepts and agrees with the following:

- Receipt of consignment of jewelry items as described in consignment product sheet.
- That the Shop will display work from Artist within five (5) days of receipt of items and will continue with displaying items for a period of **3 months** after which this agreement will be revalidated by both parties.
- That the "Store" will make every effort to obtain the best possible price for the consigned items and will accept no less than the minimum price wanted by Artist on consignment listing sheet.
- For the store efforts, they are authorized to retain **40 %** (store percentage amount) of the purchase price (before sales taxes). The Shop may buy items from Artist and may remit **80%** of the retail price to the artist instead of consignment. If the Artist accepts special orders or referrals
- That the Shop will take reasonable care in storing, handling, displaying and shipping (if required) of received items. The Shop will be liable to the Artist for any damage, loss, injury, theft or disappearance of said works in the amount equal to **60%** of the retail price of consigned items.
- After the sale of an item, the Store will forward a check for the amount of the entire purchase price, less any sales taxes within 30 days of the receipt of the same. If the Shop does not make payment to the Artist within the specified time, the Shop will pay the artist interest at **40%** per month on the unpaid balance.

169

CONSIGNMENT AGREEMENT CONT.

- The Shop shall not use any image of items for advertising without the written permission of the Artist.
- The Store will deliver to the artist on or before the end of each month (but not later than) during the term of this contract a complete statement of inventory to include:
    - The items sold
    - The date sold
    - The amount the items sold for
    - A complete list of unsold items
    - The amount of commission owed to the Shop
    - The amount of commission owed to the Artist.
- The Shop agrees to return to the Artist all unsold consigned items within _____days after receipt of a written demand from the Artist.
- The Artist will be notified of any change in ownership of the Shop and in any changes in principal personnel. Any changes in ownership/personnel will be a violation of this agreement after which said agreement will become void.

CONVENANTS/PROMISES OF ARTIST

- The Artist agrees not to place any other consigned works within a __**10**__ mile/block radius of the Shop. The Artist also agrees not to sell any items designed by Artist within the same radius.
- The Artist agrees to pay the Shop commission for any acquired work within **10** days of receiving payment from purchaser.
- The Artist agrees to repair any work that is broken or damaged due to poor workmanship or materials used free of charge. If the damage to because of customer abuse or misuse, repairs can be done upon request with a repair fee due and payable to the Artist. The Artist will decide the fee before any repairs are made.

SHOP - ARTIST ADDITIONAL ITEMS

- The Artist will retain the copyright in all works consigned to the Shop. No items may be reproduced without prior signed permission.
- The Shop may purchase any consigned items for ___60___ % of the retail price.

Signature Artist_____Date_____

Signature Shop_____Date_____

COST CALCULATOR WORKSHEET

ANNUAL DEPRECIATION - $500.00 - **Includes my computer, scanner, printer, fax, kiln, soldering equip. $5,000 total spent**

OPERATING EXPENSES/variable and fixed

Salaries	This includes salaries paid to my part time production asst., my bookkeeper/accountant. **$2100.00**
Rent	Portion of my rent for a separate studio in my house **$2400.00**
Utilities	Proportioned share of the utilities **$300.00**
Insurance	$-0-
Workshop/Studio Supplies	studio supplies and supplies to manufacture my jewelry **$6,500.00**
Office Supplies	This includes stationary, labels, **$600.00**
Advertising	postcards I printed for advertising, ads placed in a local show guide. **$400.00**
Trade Shows (craft etc)	fees and expenses for doing my yearly craft shows. **$1,500.00**
Reps Fees	I have one rep in Los Angeles. This represents the fees I paid her. **$2,000.00**
Web site fees	E-commerce fees for a shopping cart Web site **$600.00**
Postage	postcards for shows **$300.00**
Telephone	Designated business telephone **$400.00**
Transportation	Airfare to a gem show and getting to and from my local craft shows **$250.00**
Other	$
TOTAL (ANNUAL OVERHEAD)	**$17,850.00**

CUSTOM WORK STATEMENT

DATE: JULY 12,00 (current date)

Pink Polka Dot Jewelry (your co name)
11102 Pink Lane (your address
Los Angeles, Ca 90807 (your city, state, and zip code)
562-427-0000 (your telephone)

Customers   **Name:**

Address_____**City**_____**State**_____**Zip**_____
Telephone_____**CellPhone**_____**E-mail**_____

WORK FOR HIRE

Pink Polka dot jewelry **herein referred to as Artist** has been commissioned by customer above to make a custom jewelry <u>necklace.</u>

The length of this <u>Necklace will be 16 inches</u>

This piece will be designed using:

Amethyst oval gemstone rounds that measure 8mm
Swarovski crystal, Crystal color, article 5301, size 6mm
Swarovski crystal, Tanzanite color, article 5301, size 4mm
4mm daisy sterling spacers
Crystal sterling clasp

The following sketch is an idea of how the piece will look:

The total cost of this necklace is: <u>$150.00</u>
Received 50% as down payment: <u>$75.00</u>
Delivery Date: <u>November 00,0000</u>

This quote includes any resizing necessary but does not include any redesign charges. Any variations from the original description above shall constitute a redesign and will incur additional charges. I guarantee this custom work to be free of defects and with normal care it should remain in useable condition. Repairs to said piece will be made if any problems result from designer flaws by Artist and not abuse by customer.

Customers
Signature_____**Date**_____

Artist
Signature_____**Date**_____

172

LABOR & MATERIALS SHEET

This is the section where you will put what it takes to make your items. Since each item takes a different amount of time and materials, you will have to calculate every item in your collection. There are two parts on this sheet.

STYLE NAME: *ELEGANCE*
STYLE NUMBER: *1102*

LABOR: $15.00
MATERIALS: $21.00

LABOR

Number of hours to assemble	1 hour
Initial design time	30 minutes
TOTAL LABOR	1 1/2 hours @ $10.00 per hour
TOTAL AMOUNT FOR LABOR	**$15.00**

MATERIALS USED

Gems/Beads	$12.00
Findings	$ 6.00
Stringing Materials	$ 1.50
Metals	
Miscellaneous	$ 1.50
TOTAL MATERIAL COST	**$21.00**

TOTAL COSTS FOR STYLE NUMBER: _____ *$36.00*

Invoice #2345

Anyname jewelry co.
123 Hill St.
Yourtown, U.S.A.   12345
(111) 555-0000 telephone
(111) 555-0000 fax
Duns #12-345-0000

Ordered by: Wiggins' Jewelry Salon
4587 Ranch Avenue
Los Angeles, Ca 90014
(213) 555-0000

Contact person: Judy Weston
Anyrep company
1234 Sun Street
New York, NY 10000
(212) 555-1834
(212) 555-1890
Order #1187

Date ordered: 02-01-00
Shipping date: 03-11-00
Purchase #:   1106
No. Of boxes: 1
Store #:   98
Vendor #:   8879

Terms: net-30, check payable to "anyname jewelry"

STYLE NO.	DESCRIPTION	#ORDERED	QTY/PRICE	UNIT EXTENSION
152	LT TOPAZ/CRYSTAL	1	66	$ 66.00
173	MULTI-COLOR	2	75	$150.00
175	JET	1	60	$ 60.00
182	CRYSTAL	4	75	$300.00
238	ROSE/PERIDOT	6	45	$270.00
254	CRYSTAL/JET	2	55	$110.00
024	JET	2	80	$160.00
300	LT SIAM/BRACELET	3	70	$210.00

TOTAL UNITS SHIPPED............... 21
SUBTOTAL...............................$1326.00

Ground - Zone 3......4 lbs. $9.80
C.O.D.   0.00
Insurance $4.60

subtotal......... $1,326.00
shipping/insurance...... $14.40
Total:..............$1,340.40

SAMPLE COMMISSION PAYMENT FROM ARTIST TO REP

Commission payment from
November Pave
000-#0 Maple Avenue
Los, Angeles, CA
90000
01-14-00

To: Any-rep, U.S.A.
   000 Wooster Avenue
   Binja, Texas 70000

1. Invoice # 2270 Marie's salon $356.00
2. Invoice #2272 cino's accessories $358.00
3. Invoice #2285 Ben rod's accessories $259.00
4. Invoice #2286 Joan's creations $687.00
5. Invoice #2295 Vanessa's place $280.00
6. Invoice #2299 Enid's accessories $453.00
7. Invoice #2300 Martha's designs $177.00

Subtotal $2,560.00

15% commission $ 384.00

January showroom fee $ 100.00

Total due "any rep, U.S.A. $ 484.00

Paid with check #3872 dated 01/14/00.

SAMPLE SALES REP AGREEMENT

Agreement for
Sales representation

This will confirm the agreement between "anytown rep & associates (the representative) and "anyname jewelry co." (The manufacturer) With respect to display and sale of merchandise in said representative's showroom at 123 6th avenue, New York, New York, 10015. Details are as follows:

The Representative shall:

1. Display manufacturer's merchandise.
2. Send orders to manufacturer in a timely fashion.
3. Provide purchaser's credit information as needed.
4. Not be responsible for loss due to fire theft or damage.
5. Upon termination of relationship, return samples to

   Manufacturer when manufacturer is current with all monies

   Due, including orders not yet shipped.

The Manufacturer/ Artist shall:

1. Pay 15% commission on lines being shown in the showroom and, Where applicable, 20% for road sales.
2. Pay commission on the first day of the month, which is 30 days After shipping of merchandise.
3. Pay a fee of $100.00, commensurate with space provided in show-Room on the first day of each month.
4. Not do a trade show independent of showroom if showroom is Doing said trade show.
5. Pay commission on all re-orders, including those sent directly To manufacturer.
6. Pay 1/2 commission on orders canceled, due to manufacturers Inability to ship on time.
7. Send weekly shipping invoices.
8. Send the next season's line four weeks prior to official opening Date of market.
9. Retain the option of participating in trade shows or print ads offered by rep.

Please sign enclosed copy if this is in accord with your understanding of our agreement.

Anyname jewelry co. Agrees with and accepts this agreement on 01-9-00

Anyname rep co. Agrees with and accepts this agreement on 01-9-00

INDEX